Diamond Moms

Paul Savage/Savage Solutions Imaging Studios

A Mother's Guide to Raising a Baseball Player

Candace Conradi

COACHES CHOICE™

Throughout this book, the masculine shall be deemed to include the feminine and vice versa.

ISBN: 1-58518-948-0
Library of Congress Control Number: 2006920002

Book layout: Bean Creek Studio
Cover design: Bean Creek Studio
Front cover photo: Paul Savage/Savage Solutions Imaging Studios

Coaches Choice
P.O. Box 1828   ·
Monterey, CA 93942
www.coacheschoice.com

Dedication

I dedicate this book to my mother, and now guardian angel, who taught me the meaning of unconditional love and whose faith and belief in me as an author never wavered.

Author Contact Information:
cconradi@diamondmoms.com
858-592-6571 - 877-565-9031
www.legitsportsinc.com

Acknowledgments

First, I would like to acknowledge my children, Kristi, David, Lisa, and Stephen, for making it possible for me to be a mother. I could not imagine my life outside this role nor feel more genuinely blessed to be given such an honor as being called their mom. I want to especially thank our youngest son, Stephen, whose love of baseball pervaded my heart. Without his experiences, I would not have been inspired to undertake this project.

I would also like to thank my husband, Jerry, for innumerable things: his love, his patience, his support, his encouragement, and for making dinners and sacrificing our time together so I could write this book. Words seem inadequate to convey my gratitude for his support and his belief in this project. He served as a sounding board for ideas, as a baseball reference desk, a cheerleader, and my personal thesaurus as I attempted to put my feelings and passion into words.

Next, I would like to thank Tom House, for his patience, support, counseling, and continuing willingness to educate me about the world of baseball. He unselfishly donated his time, talent, and knowledge as I wrote the more technical parts of this book. I am hopeful his love and dedication for the parents, boys, and men he works with will be translated clearly through my own work. I could not have done this as well without him.

My deep and abiding thanks also go to: Tony Gwynn, head baseball coach of San Diego State University, for his many years as a Padre and his willingness to interview for my book; Geoff Miller of Winning Mind, for his friendship, his work, and his personal insights that added immensely to the quality of the information in this book; Rick Lysander, former Major League pitcher and good friend, for proofreading a book for moms; Dominick Johnson, son of former Major League player Deron Johnson Sr., for sharing his personal experience and insight as a son, player, and high school coach; Craig Weissman, scout for Tampa Bay Devil Rays; Rusty Filter, San Diego State University assistant coach; Greg Moore, University of San Francisco pitching coach, for his encouragement and support; retired head coach John Herbold (coached at California State University at Los Angeles for 25 years) for his expertise and willing assistance; retired head baseball coach Bob Bennett (coached at Fresno State for 34 years) for his advice; Gary Peale, father, for his assistance and support; and Noah Frank, student and baseball enthusiast, for his insights as a young baseball player.

In addition, I would like to thank all the mothers willing to spend hours talking to me about their experiences. My heartfelt gratitude and special acknowledgment go to

Monica Giles, mother of Brian, Marcus, Kamila, and Brandi. Her sons, Brian and Marcus, are not only accomplished professional baseball players (San Diego Padres and Atlanta Braves) but are also remarkable young men. Her advice for moms to play baseball with their sons became an underlying theme that influenced much of what I wrote. Her enthusiasm was infectious!

Thanks to Dabar Hoorelbeke, mother of Jessie and Casey, for taking time out of her busy schedule and driving to meet me for the interview. She and her husband supported their sons' baseball dreams throughout high school and college and continued to support them until they both found their way into the professional leagues. It was her inspiration that led to me to add the chapter *It's Not Over Until the Fat Lady Sings*. I felt a kinship with her, both as a woman and a mother.

I would like to thank Tracey Lysander, wife of Rick Lysander and mother to Gregory, Brent, and Kelsey. Not only was she patient as I continually drew on Rick's experience as a coach and player, she generously donated a portion of her day off to interview with me. She is a dear and treasured friend.

I cannot imagine my baseball life without the love and support of my close and long time "Diamond Mom" friends (some longer than others), Jane Allen, Ellen Stanley, Suellen Barber, Barbara Weinberg, Debby Castillitto, Rose Reilly, and Judy Peale, for their friendship, support, and open hearts. The many hours I spent with these women over the years, watching our sons play and sharing conversations, contributed to the material for *Diamond Moms* in a way that my single very subjective experience never could have. I love and admire these women and feel fortunate to call them my friends.

I would like to also acknowledge and thank my sister, Janet Diteman, who carried on our mother's torch of encouragement, urging me to write and pursue my dream. Besides being my sister, she is one of my best friends. Her love and support mean the world to me.

Special thanks go to Penny Sansevieri, my writing coach, without whom this book may not have been realized and to Melanie Rigney, my editor, who not only knew and understood baseball, but who, as my editor, kept my feet on solid ground.

And to all my dearest friends who inspire, encourage, and otherwise color my life with love, I thank you from the bottom of my heart.

Finally, to Dr. Jim Peterson, Kristi Huelsing, and the staff at Coaches Choice, I offer my very deepest and sincere gratitude for believing in this project, for taking me under their wing, and for guiding me patiently through this process. Their knowledge of baseball and their professionalism as publishers made my experience memorable and rewarding.

Foreword

It's a question I try to ask at every camp, clinic, and consulting session in which I participate around the country. "Have any of you ever seen an athlete on TV turn around and say "hi, Dad?" Obviously, they all answer "no," it's always "hi, Mom." There is a reason for this. Dads and male coaches seem to take their son's and their team's wins and losses personally and conditionally. It's probably a combination of ego and testosterone. In reality, verbal and non-verbal (body language) communication speak volumes and are, unfortunately, more often then not, negative or confrontational. ("How can you possibly do that?" "What's wrong with you?")

Moms, on the other hand, nurture their children in spite of good or bad performances, wins, or losses. They continue to attend the basic needs of their families, no matter how good or bad their sons perform. Their verbal and non-verbal communications are always encouraging, empathetic, and caring. Moms, quite simply, are more likely to be unconditionally happy, sad, or proud for their sons, not because of them.

In her book, Candie Conradi allows players, parents, and coaches to see the baseball world through a mother's eyes. She provides first-time insight and problem identification, as well as "what-to-do" solutions to many factors that often cause frustration and failure at the ballpark. She also shares the joy that comes with being the mother of a son who experiences the growth and development of his life skills, along with his baseball skills.

Diamond Moms is a great read: full of those "aha!" moments that help all of us better understand how moms in baseball can make an on-the-field difference in their sons' lives.

—Tom House

Contents

Good kids are like sunsets.
We take them for granted.
Every day they disappear.
Most parents never imagine
how hard they try to please us.
And how miserable they feel
when they think they have failed.

— Erma Bombeck

Entering the Diamond

"The more people have studied different methods of bringing up children, the more they have come to the conclusion that what good mothers and fathers instinctively feel like doing for their babies is the best after all."

— Benjamin Spock

Diamond Moms is an excursion into the "virtual" world of baseball. The information in this book evolved from several factors, including my personal experiences and my interviews with moms, coaches, scouts, and other baseball professionals. It is important to keep in mind that "personal experiences" have their factual side but are also colored by a person's subjective interpretation of each particular set of circumstances.

Some parts of the text reflect personal opinion and should be regarded as such. Other parts are based upon individual experiences (mine and others), which may or may not be the common experience for most people. And then there are the factual parts that can (and will hopefully) be easily identified.

I recognize the unique quality of each person's experiences. There will always be varying and opposing points of view. As such, our own experiences offer each of us our own sense of reality. To that end, it is my intention and hope for mothers (and even fathers and coaches) that they learn to trust their inner compass and use the road map provided within these pages as a guide, remembering that our children are our future and the greatest national treasure we have.

Introduction

"I looked on child rearing not only as a work of love and duty but as a profession that was fully as interesting and challenging as any honorable profession in the world, and one that demanded the best that I could bring to it."

— Rose Kennedy

The temperature had dropped, and the unexpected rain made everything feel eerie and surrealistic. I stood there shivering under a golf umbrella, reflecting on the past 15 years. The tarp was pulled across the infield, protecting it from the unexpected torrent that had descended upon the California landscape. I observed the scouts, coaches, and young college players, as if I was watching a movie but had somehow mysteriously stepped into the scene, an invited shadow yet somehow belonging. The men in uniform were a varied group—some tall and lanky, some shorter, some heavier, all standing in the dugout, patiently awaiting the weather's permission to play the game. A few of them kicked at the dirt, some tossed a ball into the air, some talked to their teammates. But it was dead silent, with only hints of their murmurings catching the wings of the evening air and drifting upward as if in a prayer.

The past 15 years were gone, zipping by like a bullet train. I thought of our son at the tender age of five, preparing for his first baseball experience. His hat barely fit on his little head. He appeared to be more like a hat rack in an oversized shirt. The road from t-ball to college had been filled with endless experiences, leaving wisdom and guidance in their wake. Over the years, I stumbled, fell, got up, and fell again.

As I stood there looking out on the field, wet, cold, and happy to be there, I knew why I wanted to take on the task of bringing information to mothers. I looked at these young men and realized that they were not just baseball players; they were adult men on the threshold of their lives. Many of them, as you will discover in the pages of this book, will not even play past college. The feeling of surrealism again swept over me, as if I were watching the situation from another dimension.

I had mothered our youngest son with a different style than my other three children, because he had, from a very young age, held a vision of his future. Over the years, I had felt responsible to at least attempt to make that future available to him. In this particular moment, however, I realized that my husband and I had been preparing him for life. What he needed, what all boys need, is to be prepared not for just his dream of being a collegiate or professional baseball player, but for life beyond this sport that he loves.

This very sane observation was so obvious that it embarrassed me. You are probably thinking, "Well, of course!" But when you are in the thick of the process, simple concepts are often easily overlooked or missed altogether. There is a balance to parenting. Anyone who has made pastry dough knows the quality of the dough depends upon kneading it properly. Too much kneading, and it is too tough; not enough kneading, and it is too gooey. Because our baseball-aspiring kids have a dream (something that many of us as adults have long since forgotten), it is often all too easy for parents to attach to their son's vision of baseball and either through fear or exhilaration, lose their sense of balance concerning how to deal with their kids in an appropriate manner.

The key point to always keep in mind is that in the end, your son's future is on the line, and you are the guiding light who will help him either step up to his future or get lost in it. You are his mother. You have something that other people, even fathers, have a hard time giving to him. You have the power of unconditional love.

When I was initially inspired with the idea to write this book, it came from my experience of feeling like a blind woman in a man's world, without a guide dog or white cane. It seemed to me that people were continually and deliberately rearranging the "furniture" that littered the house of baseball in which I often found myself tripping and falling. Being raised by my mother, grandmother, and aunt, my personal history had never included a male's version of life. Men's underwear was a novelty when I eventually married! So, you can imagine my surprise when I entered the world of baseball. It may as well been a planet in a far-off universe. I was a foreigner in a foreign land with people who spoke a foreign language. There were rules, written and unspoken, that continually caught me by surprise. It was my real first experience of feeling completely, wholly, and totally out of place.

Living through the experience, from Little League to college, provided plenty of "on-the-job training." I learned to enjoy the taste of leather as I often found my foot in my mouth. Even taking into consideration that I have been immersed into the male "language" of baseball for over 16 years, I am not sure that, even now, I am fluent in it. I still translate everything through my own language, the language of the heart. While I have learned the difference between what is said and what I think is said (in some instances), I have decided that it is quite all right that I speak my own language. In fact, it is imperative that I do.

So, my heart was the first voice I had when I considered writing this material. I initially envisioned this project as an outpouring of emotional guidance for the wayward moms who are more concerned about their sons' mental and physical health than whether their kids had struck out the side or hit the winning home run. Now, I see the book as a resource guide for women everywhere who find themselves in this alien universe (even if they were raised with brothers and/or had fathers who were active, present, and available). I sincerely hope that the information provided in the chapters that follow will help empower women to trust who they are and the vital role that they play in their son's life.

One of the key players in my son's baseball career has been an individual named Tom House. (Numerous references and quotes involving Dr. House and his work appear throughout the book.) A former player and currently a coach to several elite athletes (beginners through professionals), Tom told me not too long after we met: *"Your heart will break at least a thousand times before this is over."*

More recently, he reminded me that it was quite possible that I had only reached the halfway point on my journey as the mother of a baseball player. His next comments however, were deeply reassuring. They went something like this:

Mothers are the most important part of their son's journey for this reason and this reason alone: They don't care if their son strikes out the side or gives up home runs; they love their sons no matter what. No matter what.

Tom suggested that mothers offer their sons the kind of reassurance they need to survive the rigors of the sport, the kind of love that says, "It is not what you do that I love; it is who you are." *"Furthermore, never, and I mean never, underestimate the power you have in your son's life."*

And yet, there are times when we feel less than powerful. We feel awkward, and anxious, and protective. These feelings can be so overwhelming that they keep us from engaging the power we have. Being a parent is a very encompassing, lifetime undertaking. We take these beautiful young boys whose only desire is to please us and we mold them every day with our thoughts, our words, our actions…with our love.

So, what will you discover in the pages that comprise this book? You will find permission to be your son's mom. You will find resources and information that will help guide you through the somewhat muddled waters of being a baseball mom. You will find inspiration and encouragement to be a loving yet decisive force in his life. You will find solace and hope in the boy you are blessed to raise to manhood and recognize that he is, innately, an amazing human being for taking the journey he has chosen to follow.

And in the end, you will feel honored and grateful for the experience of motherhood and all it offers. Regardless of whether your son continues to play baseball past his high school or college days, you will hopefully find peace in the path you travel together.

1

Moms on the Mound

"You don't raise heroes, you raise sons. And if you treat them like sons, they'll turn out to be heroes if it's just in your own eyes."

— Walter M. Schirra Sr.

As you sit down to prepare to learn about being a baseball mom, the following declaration may seem appallingly apparent to some, but it is the main theme of the entire contents of this book and worth repeating. We are raising our sons to be self-reliant, well-adapted, responsible men. That is our job (or should be). We are not raising our sons to be baseball players. That is their job.

With that defined and out of the way, it's time to dive beneath the surface of the gigantic glacier called "mothering." Children do not come into this world with an instruction manual. It is our job to look at our sons and ourselves honestly, seeking out information that can help us be more effective as mothers. Mistakes are inevitable, and I can guarantee that you will make them. Some mistakes are easy to repair, while others can break your heart in the long term. Life has no guarantees. One of my goals in writing this book is to help you sidestep some of the bigger potholes as you progress through your son's sports years.

What I have learned from my 33 years of parenting is that there is no one in your child's life, not his teachers, coaches, playmates, cousins, movie heroes, popular icons, or media, who will have a greater impact on him than you, his parent. While other people or matters may captivate your son's attention on occasion, nothing will bring him to himself or away from himself more than you, the woman who brought him into the world. (It should be noted that in writing this book for mothers, it was not my intention to diminish the impact that fathers have on their sons. It is substantial and can certainly mold boys' lives as much as their mothers can. This book focuses on the role of mothers because, quite frankly, I am one! Hopefully, one day in the not so distant future, some insightful father will write a similar book from the father's perspective.)

As a whole, I think that mothers care too much. It is our nature to care. It happens quite by default, this sense of ownership and responsibility. We nurture and feed life from its inception, ever so sensitive to the unborn child who is developing within our own body. From the very beginning, we protect and nurture this tiny, microscopic being, giving from and through our body, unwittingly and naturally, everything a child needs to become a whole person. And once done, we continue our care by wiping noses, kissing wounds (both of the heart and body), staying up nights worrying, sewing, cooking, cleaning, driving, and carpooling to name a few. We provide and continue to give unceasingly while struggling to maintain a sense of our own purpose and identity. Yet, sensing the miraculous position we hold as women in the ongoing continuation of life itself, we simply keep on keeping on.

Like most moms, when our son was born, I was busy counting toes and fingers. My husband, on the other hand, was already thinking about playing catch with him for the first time. It's a Mars/Venus affair from the start! Those nerve-racking differences are just another reason for moms to create a place of their own in the world of baseball. Like so many things, however, being part of your son's baseball world involves the ability to exercise common sense. In my mind, good common sense is a sort of genius factor that is all too often undervalued by people.

A child's athletic talent surfaces at an early age. I find it difficult to remember a time when our son was not scooting around holding some sphere-like object in his hand. While most babies and young boys slept with teddy bears or action figures, he was sleeping with balls. He began throwing things as soon as he figured out what the hinges on the sides of his shoulders were for. And of course, they were designed to throw things. Anything. Anywhere. Any time. My interview process with mothers showed this to be true for many would-be athletes. Their aptitude for performing tasks involving athletic-related motor skills surfaced early, often by the time they were one-year old.

Many reasons exist for getting your son involved with an athletic program, elite or otherwise, as a young man. Participation in sports, as a whole, can help teach the value of discipline, leadership, and team effort. The positive side of getting your son involved in athletics at an early age is that it puts him on a path of life that emphasizes dedication and purpose. This lesson can and will eventually help contribute to his future success—in or out of sports. The negative side of his early involvement is it can lead to a sense of false value and stardom that seldom, if ever, lasts.

What begins as a simple and relatively fun endeavor when your son enters t-ball can quickly become a complex and challenging world. The process is challenging to both our hearts and our sensitivities as mothers. On one hand, we have an innate desire to protect and guide our children through troubled and confusing times. On the other hand, circumstances force us to relinquish our hold on our children and turn them over to teachers, coaches, and other adults, trusting they will do what is right for our sons. And yet, baseball (and this applies to all sports) is representative of one of the last bastions of passage into manhood for the young adult males of our world.

In reality, the world of baseball, this "man's world," is a foreign land for the moms who cross into it. It is a world where men are men. There is a language spoken within the realm called "baseball" that may as well be an ancient Chinese dialect for many women. This world requires women to understand not only the technical rules of the game, but also the underlying rules of a man's universe. Unless you were raised in an environment of baseball…unless you had brothers/fathers/uncles/cousins who played…there is a great deal to comprehend and know about baseball and sons, coaches and sons, fathers and sons. I often felt lost and unsure in my role. At times, I was very conflicted as a parent, torn between wanting to help my son grow up and my maternal need to protect him.

When we are in the thick of parenting, it is often difficult to remain steadfast in how we react to the challenges we face. And face them we will. The young eyes who look to us for guidance and care, seeking reassurance and courage, will instead occasionally see confusion and fear, especially when our sons are playing sports.

In reality, as a baseball mom, you will be conflicted. Your mind will be stretched and re-stretched. The scenario will give rise to a series of what seem to be diametrically opposed thoughts such as…

"Be there for them, but let go."

"Be involved, but get out of the way."

"Be your son's advocate, but teach him to be self-sustaining."

"Be compassionate, but be tough."

While the aforementioned notions may seem to be contradictory, they are different sides of the same coin. You will learn about the rules of the game, both on and off the field. And trust me, there are as many rules to baseball as there are to life, and often just as seemingly vague and confusing.

Frankly, I don't believe that I have all the answers for baseball moms. On the other hand, each of us has a responsibility to share our experiences with others. As the mother of a baseball player only you know where you're at on your journey as a baseball mom. When I began mine, I would have liked a road map. In essence, you are a travel agent, preparing your son for a journey, headed for a destination called manhood. Endless roads stretch out before you. Your journey will involve direct routes and side trips; on some occasions, there will be hazards, while on others, there will be thoroughfares.

Given the window of time with which you are working as a baseball mom, your best option is to take the direct route. Hopefully, the information and insights that I have attempted to share with you in this book will help enlighten you concerning what to do to successfully navigate this wondrous pathway in a way that is positive (and perhaps a bit life-changing) for you, your son, and your family.

And so, from t-ball to Little League to college and beyond…welcome, moms. And in the words of umpires everywhere…play ball!

2

The Art Of Discipline

"Moms are relentless as tides. They don't just drive us to practice,
they drive us to greatness."

— Steve Rushin,
Sports Illustrated

There is a reason that this subject is addressed early in the book. A strong foundation is vital for the success of anything we build, especially a life. Without this, no matter how strong you think the walls are, no matter how good the material (or talent), the house of the future will crumble without personal discipline. The underlying point is that loving, nonviolent discipline can go a long way to help anyone build a life that is worth living.

One unfortunate outcome to the counseling and esteem-building practices currently in vogue is that they have caused many parents to be afraid of the concept of discipline. As a result, too many parents are raising children with no sense of direction, leaving them without a firm concept of what it takes to be a grown-up person in a grown-up world. In reality, children will only respect, trust, and love themselves if they have a solid foundation of esteem, not one based upon empty praise but upon solid self-reliance. We all need to trust our choices and ourselves.

This chapter is entitled the "art" of discipline for a reason. While some people might feel that discipline is not an art form, I would heartily disagree with them. Discipline involves a certain degree of subjectivity. As such, there are as many ways to implement discipline, as there are painters who paint masterpieces. Like paintings, some forms of discipline are prettier than others, while others may be more displeasing to the senses. The one undeniable fact about raising children—especially baseball players—is that discipline must flow from life's paintbrush and that you, the parent…the mother…are the artist who is putting life's picture to canvas until your son is able to pick up the paintbrush and create his own masterpiece.

I have been around too many athletes to ignore the fact that (even in my own case) discipline is not always well-defined or implemented in an appropriate manner. Some mothers are tough and adhere to clearly set limits with their sons; others are too strict, not allowing room for their sons to make their own mistakes. However, it appears that most mothers tend to avoid the hard line until they are forced into a corner. At that point, those individuals who dance around the tough issues that inevitably rise to challenge them suddenly respond with tiger-like fierceness, startling their sons out of their socks. Eventually, some (if not many) mothers end up confused, wondering why their sons are making poor choices or why they, as mothers who have worked so hard and diligently for their sons, are disregarded or treated with disrespect.

Many women have a very difficult time stating what they want from anyone. For example, if you say to your son, "I want you to help more around the house," that is a vague and nondescript request. As such, your son's interpretation of what you really want him to do can run in a thousand different directions. Usually it will go toward the path of least resistance. He may think that turning down the television or his radio when you come into the room means he has granted your wishes. On the other hand, if you had stated, "I want you to take out the trash," your request has clarity. With regard to discipline, the key point to keep in mind is reflected in the axiom, "say what you mean and mean what you say." In fact, dancing belongs on the dance floor, not on the parenting floor. (Note: For more information on how to communicate clearly, Dr. Marshall B. Rosenberg's book, *Nonviolent Communication, A Language of Life*, is highly recommended).

Discipline is love's greatest tool and will help keep life balanced and well oiled. If used with wisdom and love, it can help parents out of corners into which we otherwise can paint ourselves. Discipline can be relatively simple when it adheres to basic precepts. As parents, it's our thinking and hearts that compromise the simplicity.

All factors considered, experience is the best teacher. In fact, in retrospect, there are a number of things that I would change as I look back over the many years I have spent being a mother. The comedian Stephen Wright perhaps said it best when he stated, *"Experience is something we get just after we need it." No wonder* hindsight has 20/20 vision.

ABC's of Discipline

Discipline involves several basic tenets that go a long way to help create the foundation for a successful life. It is not the good times that challenge us; it is the hard times. It is easy to do what you need to do when things appear to be going your way. When they don't, however, watch out. Life, like baseball, sometimes is a losing situation. Losing does not equal failure. Only in discipline is it easy to make that distinction.

You have to be willing to go to the mat on issues involving discipline. For example, one time my son (when he was very young, maybe five) said to me, "I hate you." My response was, "Well, that's OK, I love you. And if you didn't hate me once in a while, I wouldn't be doing my job." The key point that should be emphasized is that on occasion you should be your son's friend, but for the most part, it is more important to be his mother. Your self-assurance and gentle strength will become as much a part of him as the genetic code you share. You are serving as a surrogate to the most important person in his life…you are representing him to himself.

Consider discipline a painter's palette, and then let these ideas become the colors on your palette. You can personalize your own colors as you become comfortable with the process. Keep in mind that your palette contains certain primary colors. Furthermore, just as all colors are derived from combining the various basic colors, discipline is a mosaic that features a diverse array of concepts, principles, and values. Accordingly, as you are painting a picture of what your child's world can be, it is important to dip your paintbrush into the following factors so your son can see *and feel* his potential:

Integrity

Time

Selflessness (vs. selfishness)

Personal responsibility

Boundaries and limitations

Consistency

Accountability

Truth

Communication without judgment

Honesty

One step that you can take to help you remember these factors is to use the mnemonic phrase "It's PB & Catch." Associate "P" and "B" with "play" and "ball," which is exactly what you are asking your son to do, play ball with you. Once your son embarks on his post-high school journey, he is in a grown-up partnership with you. One of the challenges inherent in the partnership in the early going is that you previously held all of the cards. In the new scenario, when you have to share the playing deck, you have to take your revised role seriously if you are to be effective. Once he turns 18, he will be sitting across from you with his own cards. Make sure you are sensitive to the situation, because just as when he was much younger, you will be facing his deep (and natural) need for independence. Again, considerable forethought and sensitivity on your part are required at this point.

■ *Integrity*. Integrity involves having an unwavering adherence to your moral and ethical principles. You keep your word and your agreements. You know what you stand for, and live by the standards you set. You say what needs to be said, not simply what people want to hear. You are strongly committed to doing what you know is right. Above all else, you can be trusted.

If promises need to be broken (as sometimes they do), you should make sure that you communicate why you acted as you did, absent excuses. You should always tell the truth. Keep in mind that sometimes the deeper truth in any given situation is revealed later. In the moment, however, integrity is giving the very best you can give, owning up to your own role in any particular situation, and forgiving yourself and others when they fall short. We all fall short occasionally.

■ *Time*. There is no material gift that you can give to your children that begins to equal the value of your time. It is a gift that guarantees a return. Giving your time, when it is appropriate, can help teach your children that they have the time to do what they need to do. It tells them that they matter to you and that you are there for them. Whether it is an ear, a shoulder, or an appearance at a special event, you should always give what you can, when you can.

Sharing yourself with your children can be an immeasurable gift to them. In reality, giving of your time sometimes involves doing something that may be far less appealing to you than you would like. On some occasions, giving your time may occur from a distance. In other instances, it may be as quiet as a prayer. Regardless of the circumstances, however, it is everything. You are your children's witness to life. You should be present for them.

■ *Selflessness versus selfishness*. The concept may be shocking to you, but we all need to be selfish sometimes. As mothers, we tend to be relatively selfless, never teaching our children the true value of our time or our efforts made on their behalf. We steal from our children the ability to recognize the gifts we give to them when we drop everything we are doing to do for them what they can do for themselves. Such behavior diminishes our own value and may give them a false sense of self-importance. The reality of their "importance" will be exposed, and shockingly so, when they leave home…especially if they attempt to continue their baseball career at a high-level, Division I program. They will find out that they are not nearly as important as they thought they were.

It is important to evaluate your relationship with your son honestly. In that regard, you should write down all the things you do for him, your personal behaviors when he is involved, your lifestyle choices, and your approach to him as his mother. Then, examine how he treats you and where his expectations lie regarding you. Finally, see if your relationship with him is balanced. If it is not, I encourage you to balance it.

When you teach selfishness, you give your son permission to stand up to his peers when they are pushing him to do things that are not in his best interests. When you teach selflessness, you are teaching your son that he is part of a whole and that even the little things he does can make a difference in his life.

I was once told that in order to give, you have to receive. Overdoing either one with disregard for the other creates an imbalance that can be crippling. One of your responsibilities as a mother is to help create an opportunity for balance in your son's life. In this regard, you should encourage your son to engage in activities in which he "gives" of himself, for example, perform in community service, help around the house, etc. You should help your son forge a space in his life for both work and play. The sages had it right…there is a time and place for everything. The wisdom inherent in that counsel applies to both selflessness and selfishness.

■ *Personal Responsibility*—Another exceptional gift that you can give your son is a sense of personal accountability. Kids must learn to be responsible for their own actions. I once had a very close friend and mentor tell me that every time I pointed at someone or something else, three fingers were pointing back at me. Ouch!

Personal responsibility involves telling the truth about any given situation. A troublesome scenario cannot always be the coach's fault, the teacher's problem, or a friend's opinion. You have to have not only the willingness to embrace responsibility, but also the courage to be answerable and accountable for your actions, obligations, and personal duties. One of the best ways for a child to learn to be responsible is if you can honestly be true to yourself and admit when you made a mistake. Saying, "Wow, I made a mistake. I am sorry," can be a powerful message that can give your son permission to be human. Furthermore, it can provide a platform from which your son can reexamine and learn from his choices in life.

Don't shame your son for his faults. Just help him recognize them and move on. A cause and effect exists for all things. Eventually, given the right foundation, a bad outcome can eventually be recognized by your son as a poor choice on his part, at least in situations where he has the power to choose between right and wrong. Being personally responsible involves making choices…hopefully, the right choices. Your son makes choices every day…when he chooses his friends, decides what to eat, chooses to work out instead of watch television, or, in the extreme, says "no" to drugs. One of your key roles as a parent is to let him make choices early and often in his life and let him live with the results.

It is often said that, "What doesn't kill you will make you stronger." Given the demands and occasional incongruities of parenting, we must be strong as an ox!

■ *Consistency*—Consistency is where many people fall short as parents. This attribute can be an especially tough factor to exhibit, because you may (as I did) personally suffer and take to heart the disappointments of your children. It's so hard to watch them fall, or to keep them from having (or doing) something they desperately want to do when they must be disciplined. Your willingness and ability to act in a consistent manner can help show your son just how far he can push you. More importantly, it can help teach him how much he can "get away with" in life.

And push he will, especially if your parental boundaries are as wide as the United States. The country in which you reside with your son, collectively referred to as "your life with him," should be small in the beginning. Then, as he earns and grows into greater and greater responsibility, this "country" can expand. All factors considered, if this "country" is bigger than he is (or than he is ready for), it would only get him into trouble.

You should draw your boundaries clearly with your son. While I am not opposed to being flexible, depending on the circumstances, it is important for you to let your son know where you are willing to go and where you are not. If you believe in a curfew, for instance, make sure there is a consequence if he breaks it. Make the rules clear so he knows the size of the country in which he is living. All kids will break the rules; you should expect that to happen. Just don't undermine the foundation of your relationship with him. On the other hand, don't condemn him when he breaks the rules; just make sure that his actions have consequences that are appropriate to the situation.

One key element of your ability to act and behave in a consistent manner is how you were raised. When I grew up, I was told, "Don't do as I do, do as I say." Frankly, that never made sense to me. And guess what? I grew up doing what I learned, not doing what I was told. We are, for lack of a more refined comparison, like trained animals. We do what we learn to do.

Without question, one of the most meaningful steps you can take to influence your son to act in an appropriate manner is to be a fitting example for him. If and when you falter and your son calls you on it, be humble enough to hear his voice. As my son says, "wear it." In other words, it is OK to let your son know that being human is acceptable in life.

■ *Accountability*—When you do something you should own up to it. It's really that pure and that simple. You should hold yourself accountable and require your son to adhere to the same standard. Achieving this goal will be easier if your whole family adheres to this principle. Even if you are a stand-alone act, however, don't worry; behaving in such a way will outshine anything that might contradict it.

Accountability involves following through on your word. Sometimes that is hard to do. Accidents, illness, or any number of life's events (some people refer to them as "acts of God") can intervene and compromise your intention. Accountability entails recognizing that you are always at the beginning and the end of your experiences. Accountability does not encompass finger pointing, blaming, or victimization.

Your son's sense of accountability can be reflected in a number of ways. For example, if he has made an agreement with you to make his bed before he goes out with his friends, and he then does just that, he is exhibiting a level of accountability that can pay dividends later in his life. He may encounter any number of situations where his success will depend upon his ability to hold himself accountable for his work ethic and level of self-discipline. Doing something as small as making his bed or taking out the trash every day creates order in his routine. Symbolic, maybe, but symbolism can be a conduit for action. Sometimes, even the smallest and seemingly silly and innocuous things can mean a lot.

■ *Truth*—Mark Twain once said, "Always tell the truth. That way you won't have to remember anything!" In reality, truth can be in the eyes of the beholder. It is not always an absolute factor. Two people, for example, can observe a given set of circumstances from two entirely different perspectives. As baseball moms, our sons' playing time is one scenario where a great deal of subjectivity is often involved. As a rule, most of us, as parents honestly believe that our son is the one who plays *his* position the best, and is the one who simply should always be playing. The truth, of course, is that our son is not always the best player, even if he is an above-average athlete. The truth is that sometimes athletes need to be rested or simply need a change that motivates them. As parents, sometimes the truth can be uncomfortable or hurts. Understanding and accepting the truth is part of life. It is also a valuable lesson you can teach your son.

One step you can take to enhance your son's ability to truthfully assess his circumstances is to develop a checklist that includes such key questions as, "Have you done your homework?"; "Have you worked out today?"; "Have you done everything you can to be ready?"; etc. Such a checklist can help clearly define specific goals and objectives for your son and can help identify issues that need to be addressed. Teaching your son to answer such questions truthfully and to be aware of the fact that there are consequences if he does not do so can go a long way in teaching him to be truthful when no one is watching. The time to be truthful is always now.

■ *Communication without Judgment*—Being able to communicate in a non-judgmental manner is very difficult for most human beings. Regardless of to whom you're speaking (e.g., your spouse, your children, a family member, etc.), the most effective efforts to communicate involve clarity, reason, and focus. The words and tone of a capable communicator are an asset, rather than an impediment. Unfortunately, most critical communication comes energized with emotion and is often delivered with a sharp edge that can be cutting. Eventually, our emotions can sidetrack or completely muddle our intended message or our ability to communicate rationally. No one wins in that situation. Aggressive finger-pointing and shaming communication can leave a wake of bad feelings and remorse, which rarely brings about the desired results.

Since most people are especially emotional when it comes to their children, one possibly helpful step you can take when you're involved in a potentially "heated" situation is to share your emotional ramblings with a friend before delivering your message to your perceived adversary. Keep in mind that speaking heatedly to another adult can create bad feelings, not to mention enemies. It is never appropriate to be so invested in your opinion that you trample over the feelings and dignity of others without regard to the big picture.

The aforementioned principle applies to your son as well. Face it; all kids screw up. And when screw-ups occur, as they always do, an intense response is occasionally necessary to make the desired impression. Even in the heat of an intense moment, however, always remember when communicating with your children that you are dealing with one of their greatest fears…their fear of disappointing you.

Accordingly, when your son is not practicing as much as he should, you can be both direct and truthful, without condemning him. Getting him to look at his behavior and be aware of the probable outcomes of his actions can help him learn to face the truth (a very desirable attribute) so he can adjust his behavior or, at the very least, accept personal responsibility for it (accountability—yet another positive trait). Be honest, point out the facts to him, and then let the conclusion float to the surface like a bubble. Figuratively, it's far better to watch the bubbles float to the surface than to try and drown your son in an ocean of emotion. The only bubbles that will occur in that scenario are the ones escaping from his lungs as he tries to gasp for breath.

Too often, as parents, we mistakenly believe that we have little or no influence on our sons, especially when they reach adolescence. As a result, we occasionally try to jam our opinions down their throats. No wonder kids have been ignoring their parents' advice for what seems like forever. A love for baseball and a fixation on his performance on the baseball diamond permeate his thoughts. Whether our sons are viewing us directly or peering at us from the shadows, their young eyes look to us for guidance and care, all the while seeking reassurance and courage.

Accordingly, you should always match your words and actions with as much consistency as you can. This situation is when emotional reaction must be replaced with thoughtful, conscious choices on your part. Your decisions not only should illustrate the need and value of acting in a rational manner to your son, but also reinforce your absolute support for who he is as a person. Your demeanor and actions should not lend themselves to ambiguity. In other words, try to be as clear as a sky after a storm.

You need to be straightforward when dealing with your won. As Sergeant Joe Friday used to say on the television show *Dragnet*, "Just the facts ma'am, just the facts." One example might be, "We had an agreement (make sure you have one) that you would pick up your shoes from the living room. Please do it now." Another similar scenario might be, "You were late last night coming home. We have an understanding (make sure you do) that your curfew is 10:00 on school nights, and you didn't call." At that point, your next step should be to inform him of the consequences of his actions. Don't blame; don't lecture; and don't make him feel small for making a mistake. Just let him know that you are aware of what he has done and that you are present in his life, and then follow through.

■ *Honesty*—Honesty is truth's cousin—close cousins. Honesty is the cornerstone of character. In reality, honesty involves the relationship we have with ourselves. As such, teach your son to be honest with himself about his work ethic and his ability to exercise restraint over his actions, emotions, and desires. Don't let him lie to you or to himself when it comes to making excuses for not doing what he should be doing. It's too easy to brush off personal responsibilities with excuses, such as "I didn't have enough time," "The teacher or coach, didn't tell me," or "I didn't know."

It is the responsibility of your son to know what he should do. If he doesn't, nine chances out of 10, it is because he did not listen or ask. More often than not, when we are hungry enough for a particular outcome, we try to move heaven and earth to make it happen. Most human beings tend to think that way, even your son. It could be logically argued that hunger is a key part of the thought process in such a situation. Regardless of the circumstances, you should always try to help your son be honest with how he conducts his own life.

As your son grows up and continues to play baseball, his efforts will become more meaningful, not just for him but for you as well. Try to be honest with yourself about his ability as a player. This kind of reflection takes courage and can be challenging. A fine line exists between supporting and believing in your son's talent and acknowledging the truth of how good a player he truly is. The trouble with this concept is somewhat challenging to pinpoint as a baseball mom. I always looked to the coaches and trainers who worked with my son to tell me the truth about his talent. I simply did not know enough about the strategy and nuances of the game to fully understand what factors can make a player "good." Some elements merited more importance than I knew to give them, while others deserved less. Hence, the need for legitimate feedback from more knowledgeable sources.

If you find out from objective sources that your son is not as talented as you thought, it can take courage to be honest about the situation. It can also take courage to discern whether baseball is your dream or your son's. Ultimately, in this situation, one of the most critical issues that needs to be addressed is: Does your son want his dream badly enough to work hard enough to make it happen?

One of the best examples of the positive effect that a parent can have on his son was shared with me by Dominick Johnson, a former pitcher who was drafted into the minor league system. His father, Deron Johnson Sr., was a major league player. When I asked Dom what his dad had done that was so special, he told me he never made Dom's baseball dream his own. He never insisted that Dom hit, throw, or practice his batting. Furthermore, he had to go to his dad and ask him to throw with him, or work with his swing, or to let him pitch to him. He made it clear to Dom from a very young age that if it was to be, it was up to him. Dom's dad had it right. No greater gift can parents give to their children.

In other words, be brave and tell yourself the truth. The end result may be peace of mind. There is a great deal of peace in acknowledging and accepting things for what they are. Even though your influence is part of your son's makeup (even if you don't think so), it is *his* arm, *his* discipline, and his passion that must be engaged for him to go forward in baseball. More importantly, *his life is his to make.* You are simply giving him tools and teaching him how to use them. At some point, you have to let go and let him walk alone.

As you read and attempt to digest the information presented in the following chapters, you will see why the concepts outlined in this chapter are important. You may be fortunate enough to implement these factors naturally. For those who struggle to allow their sons the freedom to "hate" them once in a while, however, this information can be very valuable. Implementing discipline is not unlike being a pitcher. Sometimes you are alone out there, with the bases loaded, facing the power hitter. Trust me, you do not stand alone. Enjoy the strength you have as a mother. As women, historically we have often been the instigator of needed changes in the world that help make the world a better place to live. As a mother, your inherent strength extends to the influence you have on your son.

Always keep in mind that *respect* comes with *discipline*. If you think for a minute that sons hate a strong mother, simply recall whom those professional athletes are waving to when the camera zooms in for a close-up…their *mother*.

3

Packing For Your Trip

"Who in their infinite wisdom decreed that Little League uniforms be white? Certainly not a mother."

— Erma Bombeck

Questions will arise as you pack for your trip as a baseball mom. They will be simple ones that will befuddle you (much like the one in the quote that introduced this chapter) and other, more complex, serious questions. Should your son's love of baseball take him to college and beyond, you will travel a distance as wide and varied as the gap that stretches between Los Angeles and New York, filled with boundless possibilities. Your trip will involve direct routes and side trips, hazards, and thoroughfares. Road maps would be helpful. It will be critical to know where you are going, but it will be equally important to know where you begin.

So, we will start where all good road maps start, at the beginning.

As a mother and woman, you will be committing to a lifetime of sleepless nights, worry, exhilaration, fear, love, courage…Oh wait, this book is supposed to be about your commitment to your son as a baseball player.

Your level of commitment will vary, depending upon your own distinctive parenting style, circumstances, background, and personality. Some mothers are mother bears, some are hands off, some are micromanagers, and some are guidance counselors. Occasionally, some mothers are all those things wrapped into one package. Since we are all individuals, each with our own set of unique circumstances, there are no pat answers for any decision you may have to make concerning your level of commitment when it comes to your son playing baseball. Don't be fooled, however, there *will* be a level of commitment. It will be your call as to how you see your role as a baseball mom.

The baseball commitment that mothers make to their sons range between an occasional one that is based upon their son's seasonal, spring-time efforts as an athlete to the complexities that arise from being part of a yearlong program. Regardless of your son's personal involvement with this sport, there are several basic things that come with the territory.

In fact, there are a number of areas involving your role as a baseball mom that may call upon your time and/or resources, as the following (partial) list illustrates. Deciding whether you should commit to these factors (if at all) and the degree of your commitment is a personal matter. At a minimum, you have to deal with those issues that are required for him to play (such as Little League fees). It is also important that you do whatever you can to help ensure that your son can play his sport safely. Anything else is up for grabs.

■ *Schedules*. Juggling your son's schedule can be a challenge, especially if he plays multiple sports or year-round baseball. Having more than one child involved in activities (whether it is music lessons or another sport) can also complicate the task.

■ *Donations*. Youth baseball leagues are almost always in financial need. As such, your donation, which may be tax deductible, can be helpful. To determine whether a donation will be tax deductible, you should check to see if your league or program is a nonprofit organization.

■ *Volunteering.* Baseball programs are often dependent upon volunteers. Such help can come in many forms, from team moms to scorekeepers to snack bar attendants to coaches. Tracey Lysander, the wife of a former major league pitcher and mother of a baseball player, recommends learning how to score baseball if you really want to learn the game. Her advice is well taken. Likewise, coaching is another realm you should consider. If you are a woman who knows baseball and wants to coach young boys, follow your heart. Don't let baseball's traditional gender preference intimidate you.

■ *Equipment.* A list of the equipment required to play baseball and be a baseball mom is virtually endless. Baseball shoes, gloves, bats, uniforms, socks (lots of socks), hats, caps, catcher's gear (sometimes provided), hitting helmets (sometimes provided), batting gloves, laundry detergent (lots of detergent, stain remover, and bleach), air fresheners for your car, sports drinks (some are better than others), healthy snacks, ice packs, bandages, and on and on. And, oh goodness, don't forget seeds, lots and lots of sunflower seeds. They go with baseball in the same way that snow goes with skiing. Most people simply cannot do baseball without seeds.

■ *Financial.* Everything from the aforementioned list of equipment to league dues, payment for travel coaches, pictures, coaches' gifts, travel expenses (if your son plays on a travel team), lessons (hitting, pitching, base running, catching), and/or books/video/DVDs on how to hit, pitch, run, and catch costs money. The list of items that may touch your wallet is practically unending.

Brace yourself if you think no endeavor can hijack your time or billfold like golfing or fishing. Welcome to the world of being a baseball mom. The best thing about baseball, though, is it can hijack your heart. Then, all this commitment becomes an emotional roller coaster. If it does capture your heart, you will never be the same. One last thing…did I mention the sleepless nights, worry, exhilaration, fear, love, courage…?

The Journey

A baseball mom's journey, like almost all journeys, is incremental by design. Your son may begin playing as early as five years old. (Some boys start playing baseball as early as age four.) On occasion, you may even find little girls donning jerseys and playing community baseball. For the most part, girls tend to reach their physical prime by the age of 12 and rarely (actually, the word "never" comes to mind) play baseball into high school. In reality, players can normally participate in community-level baseball programs up to the age of 18. This situation offers a wonderful opportunity for those individuals who simply do not have sufficient talent to play at a higher competitive level (e.g., high school or college).

If your son makes his high school baseball team, the level of intensity attendant to the entire experience will increase dramatically. High school ball is to baseball what sun is to summer—it's hotter and more intense. Should he do well in high school as a player and as a student, it can open many doors for him, especially gateways to colleges that might not otherwise consider him for admission. Of course, for the selected few, an opportunity to be drafted professionally may arise. Unfortunately, for many young men, their baseball aspirations may conclude prematurely (at whatever level). But there are always other opportunities for them to play ball, coach, and teach. As the statistics in the next section indicate, college is where many players are either kicked off or independently make the decision to get off the bus.

Statistics

In many ways, the statistics of baseball are shocking. Every year, over 6.8 million individuals sign up to play Little League baseball. By the time they enter high school, the numbers have dropped to 2.4 million. Of the 2.4 million high school baseball players, only 70,000 to 80,000 go on to become collegiate players. Of those players, less than 10 percent (fewer than 7,000) will play professionally (initially at the minor league level), and only 750 will make the major leagues. Obviously, some of these young men drop out because they reach their peak along the way or discover that they no longer have the passion for playing baseball. For others, however, their baseball life is cut short for reasons that can be mitigated.

Dr. Tom House, a former major league pitcher and currently a coach to several elite athletes, has been a trusted and valued friend and advisor over the years, not only to our son, but also to our family. He has spent considerable time reflecting on and trying to identify what could be done to address the dilemma of a shortened baseball career that most boys encounter. His feelings on the matter are both insightful and fairly straightforward. He simply believes that "…the pyramid doesn't have to be this steep. More kids should play longer if we (as coaches) could do a little better at preparing them for the game." Frankly, the only way that will ever happen, if it ever does, is with a progressive change in attitude. The welfare of these young men needs to become the central concern of coaches *and* parents alike. Mothers can help institute the needed changes in this area.

Big dreams need an expansive, honest vision and broad shoulders to carry them. As such, big dreams are always worth pursuing to their obvious end, if at all possible. The aforementioned statistics were not included to discourage you. Rather, they are presented to help you to see the pressure that your son may be up against should he choose to make baseball one of his life's pursuits. Such a journey will require dedication, perseverance, hard work, and support—the kind of support that will buoy him when he feels he is sinking. And that is where you, Mom, come in.

4

Parent Pitfalls

*"Leaders must learn to discipline their disappointments.
It is not what happens to us, it is what we choose
to do about what happens that makes the difference
in how our lives turn out."*

— Jim Rohn

In the previous chapters, the importance of discipline was discussed, and the concepts that are important as you raise your baseball-playing son were detailed. Next, I want to cover some of those uncomfortable moments that you will encounter as a baseball mom. You know those "moments;" the ones that make you cringe in embarrassment for yourself or someone else. The ones that make even your blood vessels blush. The ones that make you wish you were anywhere else on the planet than where you are.

The information presented in this chapter is based on more than my personal observations and experiences. It also includes feedback from the many, many mothers that were interviewed for this book. Challenging times can influence our ability to think logically, carefully, and clearly. We have all made mistakes and suffered from emotional blindness. The aftereffects are not unlike an unwelcome, headachy hangover. Too much of anything is...well...not a good thing. The primary problem with the morning after (or the moment after) is not that it is embarrassing and detrimental to us personally, but that it can also have a negative affect on our sons. Pitfalls are mistakes that take you further away from the goal and when you look back, you think, "How did I end up *here* when I wanted to be *there*?"

This chapter is not intended to point out all the foibles of a parent's nature. Sometimes, parents seem to continue to do things or react in the same way because it is what they have always done. One of my favorite stories is about the newly married woman who is making a pot roast. Her husband is watching her prepare it for the oven as she slices two inches off one end of the roast. Having an inquiring mind, her husband asks why she lopped off two inches of the roast. She tells him it is what *her* mother did. They call her mother, and her mother tells them it is what *her* mother did. At that point, the young newlywed then calls her grandmother. To her surprise, her grandmother tells her it was because her pan was too short!

We often ignore our intuition. Instead, we practice what we have learned from our families or from our circumstances for reasons that no longer apply. Our reactions to certain situations are sometimes so subtle to us that while others may gape at our responses, we remain virtually unaware of their impact. Instead of wisdom, we end up passing down concepts and behaviors that are less than appropriate and effective and sometimes even hurtful.

Before you get too deep into reading this chapter, take a deep breath and give yourself a big, giant hug. In reality, we all do the best we can with the information that is available at any given time. One of the most important things to us not only as mothers, but also as women and human beings, is that we give ourselves opportunities and permission for growth.

In all likelihood, you are in a partnership with your son's father, whether or not you are married to him. Even though there are cultures that believe it is a woman's job to retrain the men in her life, I can tell you from personal experience there is a flaw in their thinking. I learned a long time ago that I could only change myself. When we surrender the antiquated concept of "fixing the other guy" and begin to focus instead on our personal growth, seemingly miraculous things can happen. It is amazing how powerfully the image of our own change can ignite the desire in others to grow. By example, one changed person can effectively change others.

Perspective

Imagine you see an All-American, freckled-faced 10-year-old, standing on the mound of a baseball diamond. In his little hand is a three-ounce sphere. Our little hero is standing facing another young boy of equal stature who has aspirations of hitting this little sphere, hurtled over the distance that separates him and our hero, as far as he possibly can. Each boy takes a deep breath, hoping to shake off the willies from his anxious little body. The ball is released, the bat attacks, and sure enough, the little sphere is hurtled through space into the outfield and over a fence.

Standing in the middle of the diamond alone, the pitcher, filled with love and excitement for the game, turns first his head and then his body as he watches the ball float over the outfielder's head and over the fence. He turns back to the mound and smiles. It was not a bad pitch, maybe a little "up," but he has the presence of mind (even at 10 years old) to honor and acknowledge the talent of the boy who has crushed his well-thrown pitch over the fence. Standing in the middle of the baseball diamond, he is center stage.

His innocence for baseball is still sugar sweet; he is playing because his heart loves the sport. He revels as the smell of wet dirt, grass, and glove leather wafts to his nostrils, spreading a silly grin across his Norman Rockwell-looking face. He delights in the feel of the warmth of the sun shining on his freckled nose. His future is right now, as he turns back to face the next hitter, who is standing anxiously at home plate. Each young man is holding love and respect for this game in his heart, as the pitcher bends his little body toward the batter. One hand behind his back, holding the leather-bound sphere, the young pitcher forgets the home run he has just given up and stares at his next new comrade who is standing at the plate. He strikes him out.

Envision this same scenario, only six-to-seven years later. This time when the ball is hit over the fence, there is no smile. The game, still loved and played with a heart full of passion, has become a far more serious engagement. College choices, weighing heavily into the equation, cast shadows over a once-light heart. The future of the young player is on the line or, to be more precise, on a hanging curve ball or a temporary batting slump. In the stands, out of reach, sitting and watching from afar, are parents, scouts, teachers, and maybe even a girlfriend.

This story is recounted only to reemphasize how much heart these kids put into what they do. As their mother, you may be sandwiched in time and space between

-year-old and 18-year-old, praying that each can successfully weather the ,es of life, including the ups and downs of baseball. While your son is standing on the baseball field, you can be assured that you and your husband, as the parents of this young man, are as much on the field as is your son. Furthermore, if the entire scenario were to be captured with a hologram, you would be able to see the shadows of you and your husband out on the diamond, hovering over your son's head, somewhat like dreams in a cartoon. Your influence may or may not be apparent to your son. Spoken or unspoken, however, it simply is part of his landscape.

A Few Words to the Wise

You may be aware of your personal Achilles' heel when it comes to your son. Just in case you are not, you may want to reflect upon the following suggestions. Many of these points were learned the hard way, if not by me, then certainly by others:

■ *Whatever your opinion, do not discuss it in front of your son.* Negative judgments, opinions, frustrations, anger, resentment, fear, or any other even mildly related opinions pertaining to your son's baseball experience should be discussed out of earshot of your son. If you are unhappy with coaches, parents, or other players, you should keep the discussion shrouded in privacy, as if you were guarding a national secret that, if disclosed, might destroy the earth. If I seem to be overstating this point, I mean to. What you have to say about your son's coach (or teacher or employer for that matter) can affect the ability of your son to work with that person. It can also influence your son's ability to realistically measure his own worth, especially in relation to the individual about whom you are speaking. Speaking negatively about others in front of your son is simply not a good practice and can tear down and destroy a team as much or more than a bad coach.

■ *Treat your son with respect, but never like a star.* The need to handle your son in an appropriate manner can be reinforced by any number of examples. Frankly, I wish I had a funny story to tell you, to illustrate this point, but as far as I can tell, most experiences pertaining to this issue are more tragically sad than funny. If you have a standout athlete, you should help him understand that his talent is a gift to be honored and respected, rather than unduly praised. I have yet to personally witness a child raised with the "star" mentality to be successful when faced off against other players of equal or greater talent. When Buddha was asked what he did before he was enlightened, he replied, "I chopped wood and carried water." When asked what he did after he was enlightened, he stated, "I chopped wood and carried water." This concept entails great wisdom. Stardom is a short-lived experience. It is critical that your son knows the difference between talent (what he does) and integrity (who he is). An injury or an accident could compromise or take his talent away from him in the wink of an eye. Furthermore, if he thinks he is a "star" and subsequently finds out that he is "average" when he is competing against athletes of equal stature, he may become so discouraged that he will give up on his dream. One of your goals should be to help him to be confident of his abilities, yet ever so humble.

■ *Earn your son's respect and then demand that your son respect not just you, but all of life.* Being respectful of others can go a long way toward creating a better life for your son. He will learn to be considerate of and show deference to others as he observes how you respond to coaches, parents, and other players. He will learn where his rights end and someone else's begins when you set clear and uncompromising boundaries in your relationship with him. The most disconcerting and embarrassing experience I've ever witnessed involved a young adolescent who was openly disrespectful to his father/coach on a baseball field in the middle of a game. In the most profane manner imaginable, he told his father to leave him alone in front of God and everyone who was within earshot. His father responded by allowing him to continue playing in the game. Although this behavior is an extreme example, other accounts of similar behavior abound. Respect is the credit card of life. The more respectful we are, the more likely it is that we will find doors opening and opportunities coming our way.

■ *Give your son responsibilities at home; don't treat him like he is a houseguest.* Lawns need to be mowed; dog poop needs to be scooped. Laundry needs to be sorted, washed, dried, and put away. Floors need to be washed, and dishes need to be cleaned and put away. Teach your son when he is young to do things that are within his ability. *I know, I know, this takes time and you don't have enough time.* What you won't have is any time down the road if you are doing for your son what he can (and must) learn to do for himself. It is important for him to have responsibilities for which he is accountable and, on the opposite side of that coin, to face consequences if he fails to fulfill his part of the bargain. Having responsibilities at home also teaches him about teamwork. I know of 18-year-old boys whose mothers still make their bed for them every day. In order to *function* in a community, you must *participate* in that community in order to feel like you are *part of* that community. More than that, participation gives your son a sense of value and is the first step on the road to self-reliance.

■ *Hold your son accountable.* Hold yourself accountable as his parent. Help your son hold himself accountable for his actions. Neither shamed nor blamed, but accountable. Teach him that for every action, he can expect an opposite and equal reaction. If he is not playing in the game, when you think he should play, teach him grace. One of the basic truths learned at this young age is that performance equals opportunity. Dedicated, smart practice can help him rise to the top if his skill level is equal to the task at hand. Teach him to have a voice, and encourage him to go to his coach with his concerns. Help his voice be strong and powerful (advice that leads into my next pitfall).

■ *Let your son have his own voice when communications need to be made to others, _especially to his coach_.* A mother's voice is powerful, and there is a time to use it and a time not to use it. Sometimes, it is necessary to make others aware of something that may be detrimental to your son or others. On the other hand, unless a danger exists to your child's health, you should not try to serve as your son's voice. Doing so can result in any number of negative consequences. You may embarrass him, interfere with his opportunities, diminish his own self-confidence, and, in the long run, damage your relationship with him.

A distinct and critical difference exists between advocacy and being an officious intermeddler. In the movie *Friday Night Lights*, Tim McGraw plays a disgruntled father who is living his life through his son. He charges the field during a practice and chastises his son in public. While this is a "Hollywood" example, even milder demonstrations of in appropriate intrusions can embarrass your son and put distance between him and you. If overwhelming feelings are pushing and pressing you to express yourself in an improper manner, try talking to a friend or family member so you can cool down. If you really love and treasure your son, remember there are times when a silent mouth is sweet to hear.

■ *Separate your own expectations from your son's and opt for peace instead.* Try not to have any specific expectations for your son from game to game. OK, OK…that may be an *impossible* request. So, try not to let your son *know* that you have expectations for him from game to game. As Tom House has often reminded me, baseball is a game of failure. There are few professions where you can make history by succeeding one-third or half of the time. (If you have a lifetime batting average of .300 or win half of the games you pitch, you can make it into the Hall of Fame.) Be at peace with this reality, and you will help provide you and your son with the perspective and grace needed to enjoy the journey.

■ *Don't try to live your life through your son.* You may be wondering why this suggestion is included in a book for moms. As mothers, we may be trying to live vicariously through our sons when we demand that they love what we love. Always keep in mind that your son's life is his to lead. Your primary role is to love and counsel him. You should encourage him to find his own path in life.

Don't allow other people to be too demanding of your son. Far too often, fathers and coaches demand an impossible level of perfection from their charges. In these circumstances, you may be the only voice of reason, reminding these adults to reflect on their unreasonable expectations. You will recognize this pitfall when it rears its ugly head, because it typically looks something like: "I cannot believe you dropped that ball…"or "I have you scheduled for nightly batting practice, four lessons a week, and to help, I have created a workout schedule for you to follow…" or "I don't care if you don't want to go somewhere else with your friends during Saturday's playoff game, you are going…" or a thousand other scenarios. When this pitfall occurs, you will know, because you will feel tight and sick in your stomach. If the situation warrants it, you must be brave and approach those individuals (a confused husband or a misguided coach) who would place inordinate demands on your son with your concerns.

■ *Once your son is old enough to have a job, have him get a part-time job.* Another way of stating this pitfall is: Don't make baseball your son's whole life—his only purpose for getting up in the morning. Most kids do their best when they are busy. It is when they have too much time on their hands that they tend to get lackadaisical about their own personal discipline. A job will help teach them how to work *for* someone else. It will also teach them about the value of a dollar and will (if the job is laborious enough) encourage them to aim and strive for a higher vision. Your son should keep in mind in any given year only 750 men will be paid the "big bucks" to play professional baseball out of the 70,000 to 80,000 who play collegiate baseball. It's important for him to have alternative plans in case his talent or passion for the sport wanes. Injuries, small or major, can also change the direction of his life at any time.

■ *Be honest and realistic about your son's ability.* Be at peace with your son's playing time. If he plays in an area of the country where baseball is a year-round activity, the competition will be tougher than if he plays in an area where baseball is strictly a spring sport. Accept your son for who he is. Acknowledge what he *does do* well and encourage him to work to improve his skills. All other factors being equal, if your son helps a team win games because he is dedicated and willing to work for his sport, he will play. When a coach has to decide between two players of similar ability, the coach will always chose the one who is working harder or has the better attitude.

■ *Be aware of the fact that sometimes change is good, sometimes it is necessary, and sometimes it is not.* You must have the wisdom to respond to circumstances as they exist, not as you would like them to be. For example, if your son is a shortstop and is playing behind a much better player at that position but second base is open, don't be unduly concerned if his coach moves him to second base. On the other hand, if your son has his heart set on playing shortstop and is passionate about his feelings, you could consider his options. If, for example, he has the opportunity to transfer to another school and be part of a program where he would be more likely to achieve his dream, you might consider allowing him to do so. At the same time, never forget that the only things certain in life are death and taxes. As you make your decision concerning whether to allow your son to change schools, keep in mind that your son will still have to try out for his new team. For your own peace of mind you must be prepared for a "surprise ending." Not all moves or steps that you might take in life will work out as planned. In this particular scenario, no guarantees exist, only differing odds of success, depending upon your son's talent. The primary caveat that you must adhere to in this situation is to let the final decision about whether your son should switch programs be your son's decision and not yours, unless, of course, it is a move based upon your family's needs, rather than one based upon your sons opportunity to play baseball. Obviously, your family should thoroughly discuss and consider the ramifications attendant to any decision about moving. A change of this proportion may not work unless your son is involved in the decision-making process. You must also make sure that such a move does not violate any rules or regulations concerning transferring to another program, particularly if your son is playing at either the high school or collegiate level. As such, you should research your local league's rules (if your son is in high school) or the applicable NCAA regulations (if your son is in college) before making any physical move. Never do anything that might make your son ineligible to play.

■ *Never criticize another player while you are in the stands watching a game.* You never know when you are sitting next to the parent, sister, cousin, or friend of the player to whom you are directing your faultfinding. In the heat of the game, there seems to be no limit to the mean-spirited things that some people will say. Comments like, "I don't know why he is in there, he is awful," can be hurtful and damaging to others. Remember, each one of these kids was once a five-year old t-ball player picking daisies in the outfield, with the same love for the game as your son. Be sensitive to the feelings of these young players. They need and deserve it. These boys can be affected by comments, even if their external show of bravado conceals their fear that you might be right.

■ *Never, and I mean never, ever ever, speak loudly enough for your son to hear your voice when he is on the field playing.* Your son may not be able to hear you as he stands right in front of you, and you ask him to pick up his shoes. But trust me, your voice is like a homing device when he is on the field. It is familiar. It can be soothing or distracting. Regardless, he will be aware of it. As such, try to keep your opinion to yourself concerning the game and your son's involvement in it. If you must share them with someone else, keep in mind that voices (including yours) can carry. Always remember who you are and where you are.

■ *Balance, balance, balance your life.* It is so easy to get caught up in the fun and furor of baseball's momentum that other things…more specifically other *people*…are sometimes overlooked. I have spoken to many mothers who regret that some people, time, and events were left behind in the wake of their life being overly involved in their son's baseball. It's not necessarily a bad thing to be so involved. Even today, I have to admit that it was and still is painful for me to miss my son's baseball outings. After all, I drove, washed, paid for, counseled, and basically mothered him through the tough times. I loved attending his games to experience and enjoy the fruits of my efforts. A day may likely come, however, when you will find (especially if your son plays collegiate ball) that missing his games will simply happen. If he goes away to college you will be experiencing them secondhand, unless you are fortunate enough to have a money tree in your backyard. It is inevitable that you will miss some of his games. And when you do, you will realize in retrospect that you missed out on some quality

time with other children, parents, girlfriends, or yourself. Never fo
balancing act—as such, make time for yourself and others.

■ *If you are personally dissatisfied with the playing time your son is getting,*
respond by making a decision to take him out of a game or off the team. There could
be any number of reasons your son could have been chosen to play on his team. In
fact, he may have been selected for a far different reason than the one you think he
was picked to be on the team. If you question the coach why he chose your son, you
should do so in a respectful manner. His response may lead you to pull your son out
of a game or tournament or season because you think he is a better player and the
coach simply cannot see it. If you take such an impulsive action then you are teaching
him that 1) it is OK to walk away from a commitment, 2) he is not part of the team,
but an individual player, 3) he is somehow better than he thinks he is, and 4) you will
always bail him out of a situation with which he is uncomfortable. While this particular
set of circumstances could involve many other subtle points, it is important to realize
that while you may be thinking you are "standing up" for your son, you are really
"standing in" for him.

■ *Beware of sending an unintentional message of entitlement to your son.* Every
baseball mom should look closely and honestly at her situation and determine whether
she has sent the message of entitlement to her son. Too often, young athletes have
such an unwarranted expectation, which can unintentionally result from interactions
with their parents, including subtle messages from them that may otherwise seem
innocuous. Just because your son is a great athlete does not mean that he "deserves"
anything. Often, when we "think" we deserve something, we have not earned it. As
human beings, we are entitled to certain things (as Thomas Jefferson so aptly put in
the Declaration of Independence): life, liberty, and the pursuit of happiness. Everything
else requires work. As conventional wisdom so succinctly implies, "there is no free
lunch." A sense of entitlement can steal an individual's future faster than plague steals
that person's life.

■ *If you donate your time, talent, and money, don't do so with the expectation your*
son will receive playing time. In reality, some people are more inclined to serve than
others. Statistical evidence indicates that only 20% of the population of any one group
constitutes the core contributors, be it money, talent, or time. You should be saluted if
you fall into that segment (20%) of the population. Many organizations would fail
without the effort and hard work that you and others like you so generously give. On
the other hand, if you are inclined to volunteer, do so from your heart, not with an
ulterior motive, particularly in a misguided attempt to garner more playing time for your
son. It rarely works, and you may feel angry, hurt, and disillusioned when things don't
turn out the way you think they should.

Pitfalls a Plenty

In reality, an entire book could be written on the subject of the potential pitfalls that baseball moms are facing. I am sure that you could personally add to this list; we all have personal stories that, when told to another, the response is: "NO WAY!" It's so easy to look at other people making the blunder and cringe at the thought of what they are doing.

With regard to the difficulties and "traps" that you may ultimately encounter as a baseball mom, pay attention to your situation. Be aware of how your actions can affect others (particularly your son) and how you may be affected by the behavior of others. Be kind to yourself, but be honest. If you should fall into a pit, just stand up, dust yourself off, apologize if you need to, and move on.

5

The Winning Philosophy—
Mind Over Matter

"I don't understand why a team that comes in second place is called a loser.
If they are doing it, playing the game, then in my mind
they are all winners."

— Jackie George, my mom

There is an adrenaline rush that comes with winning. Boston is still reeling from its World Series win in 2004. Having been in a "winning drought" for many, many years, the win was even sweeter. The Red Sox fans are devoted; they love their team and hate the Yankees (a mutually shared attitude). Since the fall of 2004, they have been on the top of their game. They have broken the curse. Their achievements represent success not only to the players on the ball club, but also to every citizen of Boston (and every other devoted Boston fan).[1]

Winning represents success. In turn, success represents power and helps propel us to move forward toward our dreams. We live in a country where success or failure often defines us as human beings. Baseball is no different; success or failure can define the future of the player. In reality, not all losses are viewed as failures. On the other hand, a succession of failures by any particular player can result in that athlete losing his position. For a very few gifted athletes, it can make the difference between signing a contract to play professional baseball for millions of dollars or buying lottery tickets and hoping to win a million dollars.

Given a choice, we would live in a utopia where my mother's concept of winning was a reality, but we do not. As baseball moms, it is somewhat painful to watch the "agony of defeat" that is displayed on our sons' faces and in their behavior as they deal with the negative circumstances that occasionally confront them on the diamond. Over time, you will learn that your son's baseball experience will feel "bad" more times than it will feel "good." The key is what you do in situations where your son feels "bad" about his situation, particularly when it involves his personal performance.

Winning Minds

I reached a point in our son's high school baseball career when I had neither the understanding nor the knowledge to respond appropriately to his struggles. Not that he had that many, but it was painful for me when he would lose a game. I always knew he loved baseball more than anything else he did. Subsequently, those moments when he was forced to grapple with his circumstances showed me how devoted he was to the game. I also hated seeing him agonize over the challenges imposed by his sport. One of my greatest fears was that somehow those demanding hurdles would rob him of his dream to play.

Even though we were fortunate enough to have a substantial support base to help him in his troubling times, I recognized that he needed an objective person with whom he could talk, because, quite frankly, my voice was the last one he wanted to hear. Not because he didn't respect what I had to say, but because I was simply too close to the

---

1. Babe Ruth played for the Boston Red Socks (sic) until 1920 when the owner of the franchise, Harry Frazee, sold him to Colonel Jacob Ruppert, then the owner of the Yankees. Up until that time, the Red Sox were the hottest team in baseball, having won five straight World Series championships. Babe left Boston and so did their winning streak. They did not win the World Series again until 2004. Many people believed the Red Sox were cursed because of the sale.

situation. Furthermore, I was not objective. As such, I felt like a deer in headlights. move and had no words left to say. I was powerless to help my son with his circumst

At this point, Geoff Miller and his company, Winning Mind (a San Diego-based, h performance consulting group), became part of the scenario. With a degree in spor psychology, Miller had the emotional detachment and training that would turn out to be extremely helpful to addressing my son's situation (how he was able to lend a hand will be covered later in this chapter).

One of Geoff's initial comments to me was that, "he would probably win a Nobel Peace Prize if he could figure out why kids didn't listen to their parents!" Sometimes, we all need an objective set of eyes and ears to help guide us through life's obstacle course. The value of bouncing ideas off someone who understands not only the nuances of the game, but also their practical applications to day-to-day life should be recognized.

Think about it for a moment. Would you go to a computer technician to learn how to fix your car? Sometimes, we are the computer technician when it comes to dealing with our children.

If you have reached an impasse with your son in helping him overcome adversity, there is no shame in asking for help. In fact, it may be one of the most courageous things you can do. You always know when someone is struggling mentally on a baseball field. You can see it in how he plays. While even the mentally tough will succumb to doubt, it seems they have fewer moments of doubt than others. It can be argued that mental self-discipline is as important as physical talent. In fact, these two attributes are integral to each other. When they are working together, you have a dream scenario—the rest is up to fate and circumstances.

An Important Role

You may be wondering how your role as a baseball mom can help your son develop the requisite level of mental toughness. In this regard, your function entails part awareness and part communication. Furthermore, it involves keeping your definition of "winning" in proper perspective and being able to serve as a model of emotional stability to your son when times are tough for him.

One of the terms used in baseball is called "framing the ball." If a catcher can "frame a ball" successfully, he can help create an image of a strike instead of a ball if the pitch is close. Catchers who can frame the ball well are highly regarded. The term also has relevance for your role as a baseball mom. If you can learn to "frame" a situation so it is perceived in a more appropriate light for your son, you can help him immeasurably. For example, if your son made an all-star team as the last player chosen and subsequently doesn't see a lot of playing time, you could remind him what an opportunity it is for him to be part of the team, rather than allow him to feel victimized

e.

...ind and training have led him to believe that any player's ...to his own expectations. As baseball moms, we can help ...situation as a simple isolated event, rather than a set of ...s that define a future that is still well in front of them. One ...his clients to do, and one that every mother would be well ...adopt, is to be realistic about their expectations concerning their children and then to deal responsibly with any situations that may arise when those expectations are not met. Miller's Winning Mind philosophy recommends "the best way parents can help their kids with that struggle and with that pressure is to help them understand how to be OK with whatever *their best effort is, regardless of the result."*

Too many individuals measure their own success as parents by how well their children perform in a particular endeavor, such as sports. In these situations, parents subject their children to a definition of success that is inappropriate and misplaced. Not surprisingly, these parents are too often willing to share their reaction to a sports outing gone bad with their sons—a situation with innumerable pitfalls for the emotional health of these young athletes.

As a baseball mom, you should try to separate your dreams from the ones your son has. It is hard enough for him to carry his dream of tomorrow on his shoulders, let alone dealing with your expectations of his performance. Just love him and celebrate his efforts. When it comes to "winning" and "success," that is all he needs or wants.

It could be argued (ill-advisedly) that this particular approach advocates, "it is OK to lose." While losing is certainly no walk in the park, it is also not the end of civilization, as we know it. Like it or not, "lose happens," just like "poo happens." In reality, it is not *what* happens that matters; it is *how we handle what happens* that is important. If our sons see long and depressed faces after they have personally had a bad game or their team has lost a contest, they may begin to dread their experience and journey as ballplayers and not enjoy the moment. Even worse, perhaps, they may start to doubt themselves. Eventually, the situation may have a negative impact on both their level of mental toughness and their ability to perform up to capability dictated by their God-given talent on the field. Such a scenario could also affect their future in unintended ways. You should be empathetic with your son's *feelings*. You should maintain a soft smile on your face, as you pat him on the back and help him navigate the obstacles he perceives to be in his path. Keep in mind that it is about the journey. Life is always about the journey.

Emotions—the Language of Life

Emotions are the songs of the heart. Sometimes, they are sweet, melodic melodies that move us to grateful tears; other times, they are like fingernails on a blackboard.

But they are part and parcel of the human experience. Your son will have them, and he will have them on a regular basis, especially during baseball season. It is important that you allow him to have particular heartfelt feelings as long as he expresses them in a reasonably healthy way. For example, pouting and sullenness are acceptable to a certain degree, while hostility and malicious intentions are not.

The following scenario can help illustrate the array of emotions that can result from a particular situation. Imagine you are hosting your family's Thanksgiving dinner and you have worked for weeks and weeks to prepare it. You have just spent 12 hours in the kitchen, cooking the turkey, making dishes, setting the table, and ensuring that everything is exactly as you want it. Everyone has arrived, and you are center stage. The house is beautiful; dinner smells fabulous. You take out the turkey and set it on the counter in the kitchen. Everyone files in to the dining room, and while you are away from the turkey, your sweet but totally clueless dog jumps up on the counter and pulls the turkey onto the floor. In that setting, it is quite natural that you would be emotional. In fact, you might be inclined to give the dog away. Just don't go chasing him with a butcher knife!

A different scenario, but one equally relevant to the point that emotions often can arise in any given setting, involves your role as a baseball mom. Your son is pitching, the bases are loaded, his team is up by one run, and a kid on the other team comes up to the plates and hits a home run. The most significant difference between the first example and the second scenario is that in the second situation, there is no dog to blame.

Even if you have a healthy perspective on winning and losing, you will find that emotions are just part of the game. In reality, emotions take time to smooth themselves out. Nothing lasts forever, especially a loss or a bad game; tomorrow will always come. Eventually, everyone will recover from their emotional valleys. If they don't, then it is time to get professional help.

Emotions move us, hopefully, to examine our lives and enable us to infuse our life with a measure of much-needed passion. Personally, I wouldn't change any of my emotionally charged moments (and I tend to be a pretty emotional person). What I would change as a mother is my perceived need to take my children out of their own emotional whirlwinds simply because I was in personal pain while witnessing their own sense of emotional trauma. I would let them deal with their sadness, disappointment, and sorrow by themselves until they were ready to talk about it. Then, I would be there for them, withholding judgment and advice, unless asked to provide it. (Something I am still learning to do).

Keeping a Proper Perspective

As a baseball mom, it is essential that you never allow losing to equate to failure in your mind (or your son's). If it feels like you may be doing so, you need to redefine what failure means to you. In that regard, you should consider the meaning and application of the following quotation to your value system:

"Failure is, in a sense, the highway to success, since every discovery of what is false leads us to seek earnestly after what is true."

— John Keats

If you examine what success means to you, you will undoubtedly discover how you are defining and teaching success to your son. Such an examination will involve asking yourself several important questions, for example, "How do I (or your son's father) react to success and failure? How do I speak of it when my son is around? How do I mitigate the effects of a partner whose language (whether spoken or unspoken) clearly communicates the misguided concept to our son that he is "such a loser?" What actions do I take when I see my son's heart or thoughts melting him down?" Effectively dealing with this situation mandates that you adhere to the five "Bs": be aware, be consistent, be honest, be strong, and be present when your son needs you.

If your son is young, you can teach him that winning or losing is not what really matters in life; rather, it is the effort he puts into what he does that really means something. If he is older and you wish that you had dealt differently with him concerning this issue, it is never too late to start doing the right thing. You might have to break down some degree of mistrust that may arise between you and your son regarding this matter, but eventually he will reconsider his (and your) viewpoints. If you are sincere in your approach, he will respond in an appropriate and positive way.

Most mature adults accept the fact that sometimes the results we want to experience in life do not occur. Disappointment is simply an occasional part of the dynamic design of our universe. When we don't "succeed" and the definition we subscribe to concerning success involves who we are, rather than what we do, then we tend to beat ourselves up. On the other hand, as a baseball mom, if you define "success" in more quantitative, absolute terms (e.g., your son's final score of 5-4), then you have framed success as a particular moment in time. As such, you are free to move forward to encounter the next set of circumstances in your life, unencumbered by a shallow, dysfunctional definition of success. And you can be assured that eventually success will follow loss much like the sun follows a rainstorm.

6

Stay Off Bandwagons

"A silent voice is sweet to hear."

— Taken from *A Thousand Paths to Wisdom*

Banding together to collectively strive for a greater good is a powerful concept that can change the world. No one better reflects this point than Martin Luther King Jr., when he spoke to thousands of people in Washington, DC, and delivered his "I have a dream" speech. His words were powerful and mesmerizing and awakened an inner voice in most people that spoke to equality and fairness among all peoples.

The other side of the coin was Adolph Hitler, whose vilifying words and invocations to action exhorted his countrymen to engage in horrific deeds against others. One of the primary differences between Martin Luther King and Adolph Hitler is that one individual spoke to the hope and basic goodness in humanity, while the other person spoke to fear and the worst attributes of mankind. The aforementioned help illustrate how emotion can push people into action.

Baseball obviously can be a very emotional sport, a trait that offers both an upside and a downside. On one hand, your emotions can help reinforce your love and passion for the game. On the other hand, your emotions can cause you to engage in actions that can embarrass your son, your family, or yourself. The following story from my early years as a baseball mom demonstrates the ominous impact of emotions. Our son was a member of a traveling baseball team that was playing on a cool summer night. As a general rule, we always had two umpires for our games. On this particular night, however, we only had a plate umpire who was, by all measurable and objectionable standards, not very consistent or accurate. I don't recall if my son was pitching (I would like to remember him NOT being on the mound). As the game progressed, it seemed obvious to us (the parents) that our team was not getting any breaks from this umpire. In response, we began taunting him, in some cases, unmercifully. By the end of the game, we had worked ourselves into such a flurry that the guy ran for his life. He called the last out and, lickety-split, was in his car and gone.

Looking back, the thought mortifies me that we would have demonstrated such horrible sportsmanship. (I would most certainly apologize to the poor man if I could). At first, we all felt somewhat justified that we had caused him some fear. Not too long after the game, however, I began to reflect on our behavior—specifically my behavior, and I vowed to never again allow other people to influence me to act in such an unseemly manner.

You represent your son and your family wherever you go. As mothers, we are ambassadors for our family. When we behave in inappropriate ways, we are not simply "expressing ourselves." Rather, we are reflecting a picture to the world of our family's private life, even if it is only a partial portrait…all the more reason to maintain our dignity.

There are times when we see what we see, and what we see is personally offensive to us. In reality, our perceptions are often on the mark. In turn, it is hard not to feel somewhat victimized in a situation where our fate hangs on the subjective opinion of someone else, as was the case with the aforementioned umpire.

How we handle stressful moments is what matters the most. Life is the stuff that memories are made of and what we make of them. Unfortunately, some memories (e.g., my memories of the umpiring experience) can leave a poor taste in the mouth. Obviously, we could have handled the aforementioned situation in a much more dignified and graceful manner. Unfortunately, we did not, and I regret it.

Even if that individual was the worst umpire on earth, we had acted like an overzealous mob. Although we would never, as a group, have physically accosted him, he felt unsure and unsafe. How stupidly we behaved over one silly meaningless game, which did not affect our "record" and was not tournament game. Even if the game had "mattered" for one reason or another, unkind behavior of this type is unnecessary, unkind, and ugly. The guy was out there doing his job, and we did not accord him (or his position) the fundamental consideration and courtesy that he deserved. Worse yet, we did not teach our sons much about respect or accountability that night.

The key point that must be emphasized is to stay off bandwagons. You just get dusty and dirty along the way.

7

The Coaching Quotient

"A leader, particularly a teacher or coach, has a most powerful influence on those he or she leads, perhaps more than anyone outside the family…helping to mold character, instill productive principles and values, and provide a positive example to those under (a coaches) supervision…It is a privilege (not) to be taken lightly."

— John Wooden

I am deeply grateful for coaches. The majority of the individuals who coach baseball do it not only for the love of the game, but also for the love of the players they coach. Volunteer baseball coaches donate countless hours of their time, energy, and talent to provide opportunities for our baseball-playing sons. Even coaches who are paid typically receive minimal stipends, especially high school coaches. Most college coaches usually earn a modest annual salary, while a few are relatively well paid at the more prestigious schools. Regardless of where they are employed, none of them are "making a killing," and all of them work well over 40 hours a week during baseball season. There may be a few baseball coaches who work for a paycheck, but that segment of the coaching fraternity would represent a very, very small minority of those individuals who coach baseball.

A good coach can inspire a player to play well. A great coach will take a good player and inspire him to play at his highest level. A phenomenal coach will teach our sons how to be successful, on and off the playing field. Unfortunately, there are as many ways to coach as there are to parent. It's that human element of baseball that we all love and, in the same breath, criticize and even loathe on occasion. In the presence of a great coach, we feel blessed and maybe even awed. When we encounter an incompetent coach, we only need one thing…tolerance. Regardless of any coach's style as a leader, it is important to remember he is continually in the foreground, making decisions he must stand by despite the concerns and opinions of others, particularly the parents of his players. Given the passion that parents feel for their children, coaches often have to deal with hostility and adverse circumstances.

As mothers, we know that it's easier and much less challenging to parent talented, well-behaved, compliant kids. In reality, being a coach is no different. As a parent, however, you must face the fact that as parents, we cannot give our children away (although on occasion, it may have crossed my mind, if only for a millisecond). Coaches, on the other hand, get to pick and choose. Accordingly, your son needs to realize that while he has unconditional love at home, it is unlikely he will on the baseball field.

What Coaches Look For

First perceptions are everything. In fact, they impact many of the judgments that are made on a daily basis. They can also influence the opinions that a coach forms of your son. In that regard, two factors typically have a bearing on the initial impression that your son makes on his coach: talent and attitude.

Coaches of all sports, at all competitive levels, are always looking for talented players. Baseball is no exception. Coaches "see" your son's playing ability, whether by personal observation or through written or verbal feedback from others. More often than not, particularly in the youth leagues, an evaluation of a player's "talent" can encompass more than how hard he hits or how well he throws a ball. It also entails such factors as whether he seems to be a quick learner, does he move naturally (as opposed to moving as if his body constantly gets in his way), how much and what kind of coaching has he had to this point in his baseball experience, does he appear to have a natural instinct (feeling) for the game, etc.

In addition to talent, coaches look for a good attitude in their players. As a desirable attribute, a suitable attitude takes a backseat to talent by only a split hair. Early on, especially in Little League, most coaches place a lot of emphasis on the level of enthusiasm that a player exhibits, hoping all the while that his skills are sufficient for the task at hand. Rick Lysander, a former professional baseball player, father, and coach, once told me that when he chose kids for his teams, he would put the initials "WTP" next to some names. "Wants To Play" is not just a Little League acronym; it is an attribute coveted by coaches at all competitive levels in their players.

All coaches want their athletes to be passionate about and dedicated to their sport. As a rule, most coaches are often able to see such passion and dedication in their players, even when no one else notices. The importance of these factors should not be underestimated. In fact, most coaches are like Rick Lysander. When it comes down to choosing players for a team, a coach will always select the player with a "WTP" attitude, especially when deciding between two players of equal playing ability.

It is essential that you communicate to your son how consequential his attitude can be. Not in a blaming way or in a "this is how you do it" way, but in a "this information is very important for him to know way." For players who are good but not great or outstanding, it is absolutely critical that they understand the impact that their attitude can have on their baseball experience. Athletes who need further confirmation should reflect on the words of Tony Gwynn[1], future Baseball Hall-of-Fame player and currently head baseball coach at San Diego State University. When asked about what kinds of factors he looked for in players, he offered the following response:

- Their ability to play in their position
- How well they know their position, whether they are "smart" baseball players
- Their composure on the field
- Their level of hustle
- Their appearance (do they wear their uniform neatly; is their hat straight on their heads; are their shoes shined; and is their hair neat?)
- Their level of self-motivation

---

1. Tony Gwynn played two sports in college and was eventually drafted into professional baseball. As a professional baseball player, he played right field for the San Diego Padres from 1982 to 2001. Unlike many players today, Tony Gwynn made the Padres his "home" his entire baseball career. He won five Golden Glove awards, seven batting titles (Silver Slugger awards), and was voted team MVP multiple times. Based upon his career he will most certainly make the Baseball Hall of Fame within the next few years. (Players need to be retired for five years to be eligible for nomination.)

What most young men don't realize is that many of the individuals currently coaching are much like Tony Gwynn: "old school." Baseball, especially at the college and professional levels, is serious business. When coaches and scouts are recruiting, certain attributes, such as a player's attitude, are valued and easily observed.

As a baseball mom, there is something else that you should know. Coaches and scouts often sit in the stands, incognito, wanting to see the "real" players on the field. This scenario often involves the "real" parents in the stands, as well. Accordingly, you should always behave in an appropriate manner; you never know who may be sitting next to you.

The Good, Bad, and Ugly—Individuals who Coach Youth Players

Good and bad are relative terms. For example, with regard to coaching, a person can be a "good" coach for one individual's son, and yet inadequate for someone else's son. Several general guidelines exist that can help you determine what type of coach may be better suited to your son. These measures can be especially useful when you are in a position to choose your son's coach. For example, you should always consider your son's personality when trying to match him up with a coach (for independent lessons or for travel teams). Eventually, however, (short of your son being abused physically) your goal should be to help your son make every experience he has with coaches a positive one, even the more challenging ones.

Before reviewing what is good, some misconceptions need to be addressed. "Good" is not a coach who speaks kindly and treats the team as a democracy. (Our sons need leaders.) "Good" is not the coach who favors your son because your son has a demonstrable level of talent, but ignores his job with the other, less talented kids. (Our sons need proper perspective and evenhandedness.)

Both effective and ineffective coaches tend to exhibit certain attributes. The key is to know which is which and to be able to recognize the difference. Even that may not be enough. As baseball moms, we are sometimes caught in between a person's level of effectiveness (or lack of effectiveness) as a coach. Given our overriding desire to protect our sons, a coach's perceived inability to behave as we believe he should can be very difficult on us. Furthermore, we feel that such a scenario only has a downside for our sons. Not true. For example, some parents are under the illusion that their son is not learning something from "poor" coaching. Sometimes, he learns more.

Even with great coaches, you may find yourself on a roller coaster ride as the mother of a player. If you want to gain a better understanding of what a "good" coach might look like, you should watch the video, "John Wooden: Values, Victory, and Peace of Mind." John Wooden was an exceptional coach and is an even more remarkable man. He coached the UCLA men's basketball team for 27 years, ringing up a string of championships and creating championship players in unprecedented numbers.[2] After he retired, he helped companies and businesses do strategic planning, based upon his coaching concepts. In the minds of individuals everywhere, this man should be voted coach of the century, maybe even of the millennium. From a mother's perspective, he should be cloned.

Traits of "Good" Coaching

■ *Demanding*. A good coach is relatively tough on his players. He demands a lot of them. He requires that they act and play in a disciplined manner. He challenges them to have a strong spirit. He compels them to work on fundamentals over and over again. He exhibits an unwavering commitment to preparation, so that when game time comes, his players are prepared to do what they have been trained to do. He implores his players to honor and be responsible for their "home" (i.e., their team's baseball field). Demanding coaches hold their kids accountable for their behavior and work ethic. Tough coaches demand and earn respect from their players.

■ *Balanced*. In the developmental leagues, a coach with an appropriate sense of balance ensures that every player on his team gets a chance to play. Of course, this situation changes as your son progresses on his baseball journey. In competitive leagues, coaches play the athletes who work hard and earn their spots. These coaches seldom promise one thing and then do the exact opposite. They never bad-mouth other players in front of their teammates, especially if the player they are criticizing is out of earshot. Instead, they directly confront the player in question and detail what he can do to improve. They are honest with the player about his areas of weakness and offer candid guidance and instruction toward improvement.

■ *Honesty*. Honest coaches do not pull punches with their players. If a player is not being played, they make a reasonable attempt to help the player understand why. If the player is layered deeply in a roster (i.e., there are more talented players with seniority who play in front of them), they inform this player of this fact. On occasion, they might even suggest or help a particular player to be placed on another team if the player makes such a request. It could also mean that your son might choose to play an extra year at a given competitive level (as opposed to moving up to a higher level) so he gets needed playing time. Nothing beats real game experience. Sitting on the bench is no way for a player to improve his skills.

---

2. John Wooden amassed an unprecedented string of accomplishments over his coaching career, including:
- Ten NCAA men's basketball championships
- Seven NCAA championships in seven consecutive years: 1967, 1968, 1969, 1970, 1971, 1972, and 1973
- The most appearances in the Final Four, 16; most consecutive appearances in the Final Four, nine; and most victories in the Final Four, 21
- The most consecutive victories: 88 during 1971, 1972, and 1973
- Thirty-eight straight victories in NCAA tournament play between 1964 and 1974
- Four perfect seasons: 1964, 1967, 1972, 1973
- Eight perfect PAC 8 (now the PAC 10) Conference seasons
- An all-time record 40-season winning percentage .813 (Dayton High School, South Bend Central High School, Indiana State Teachers College, and UCLA).

■ *Equitable*. Fair and equitable coaches treat every member on their roster as having equal importance. Such an attitude may be very difficult to adhere to when a team has one or two outstanding players. An evenhanded approach can help give the team and any outstanding players on it, perspective. Like it or not, we are all expendable.

The word *excel* is defined in *Webster's Dictionary* as "to be distinguishable by superiority." Hopefully, we all reflect that attribute to a certain degree. Some of us need to dig a little deeper than others to bring it to the surface. A coach who can demand or elicit exceptional achievements from all of his players (as opposed to just a few) is a gem. Such an individual is a "Diamond Coach"—a person who is able to bring the best out of any player, no matter the level of his athletic ability.

Larry Brown, the head basketball coach of the New York Knicks, is a member of the advisory board of the Positive Coaching Alliance, a Northern California-based organization that is dedicated to promoting value-oriented coaches. When interviewed by *USA Today*, Brown was asked if he treated A and B players on his team differently. His response reflects his belief that coaches should treat their players in a fair, impartial way. According to Brown,

> "…The one thing I know is if your best player has great character, the chances of succeeding are incredible. If your best player is not of good character, then you have a problem. If you treat the best players differently, that is noticed by the other guys. Best players can get rewarded with the most money and public adulation, but in the locker room and on the court, they are part of the team. From the best player to the 12th man, you make them understand that you want to make them the best they can be. You're not being fair to them if you don't work with them to reach their potential."

Excelling should not mean winning. Rather, excelling involves becoming all that you can be. A coach who recognizes that precept is more likely to try to draw the very best out of each individual on his team. In turn, his athletes will play well, and his team will do well. A coach like this is the answer to every diamond mom's prayer.

■ *Integrity*. A coach with integrity will keep his word. Among the more common synonyms for integrity are virtue, honor, and morality. A coach who has integrity is strongly committed to doing what he knows is right, both for the team and his players. He sets and abides by standards that are grounded in his moral and ethical principles. Players on his team who are concerned about what their coach would want them to do in a particular situation should look to those standards for guidance.

■ *Concise, clearly communicated boundaries*. The previously referred to John Wooden video includes a story that helps illustrate the point that coaches should set straightforward, clearly communicated behavior boundaries for their players. During Wooden's illustrious career, he attracted many high-level players to his UCLA basketball team. Bill Walton (who eventually went on to play in the NBA) was one of those players. Paraphrasing the story on the video, Walton recalled that Coach Wooden had a rule that all players had to have clean-shaven faces. During the 1960s, which was a time of burgeoning free expression, Walton showed up at practice one day after a 10-day break with a beard. He informed Coach Wooden that he felt that he should be allowed to wear it—that it was his right. Coach Wooden asked him if he really believed in it that strongly. To which Walton replied, "Yes, I do, Coach. Very much." Coach Wooden replied that he "had a great deal of respect for individuals who stand up for those things in which they believe." He then told Walton, "The team is going to miss you." Needless to say, Bill Walton shaved his face clean. Wooden's boundaries were clear. Walton knew where he stood with Coach Wooden.

John Wooden knew who he was, and what his true purpose was as a coach. Furthermore, he seemed to be able to translate that message to his players. It is not surprising that most of the individuals who were fortunate enough to have played for him continued to experience success in their lives even after their playing days had ended.

The aforementioned picture painted of the "ideal" coach may be somewhat unrealistic. Obviously, not every coach can be Larry Brown or John Wooden. What they can be, however, is demanding, fair, and value-oriented. On occasion, such coaches may seem to be unreasonable. On the other hand, being perceived to be unreasonable may be nothing more than a by-product of a healthy dose of truthful candor. Sometimes the truth, while unbearable, may need to be said. In my opinion, my son has learned more from his coaches who were demanding than from the individuals who just wanted to be his buddy. In reality, diamond moms can learn a lot from talented, value-oriented coaches who truly care about their players.

What to Do

On occasion, your son may end up on the short end of the coaching experience, instead of with a competent coach (or even a poorly trained coach). It can be very challenging for you to teach your son how to cope and deal with a coach who is hard to take (for whatever reason). It is important to teach your son that life often offers up unavoidable challenges, seemingly on a daily basis. How your son addresses the challenges in his life *will* impact all facets of his life—from his experiences on the baseball field to his relationships with others off the field.

If your son's coach has a coaching style or manner that is difficult for you to stomach, you may have alternatives. Before you take any action, it is essential that you don't respond in a knee-jerk fashion. Initially, someone should talk to the coach about the relevant concerns. If your son has not reached high school age, the task of addressing the coach may appropriately belong to you or his father. Even then, unless the issue is of a very serious nature, you should ensure that your son is an integral part of the process. In all honesty, however, most coaches (even youth baseball coaches) typically will have no interest in your opinions.

If your son is older (i.e., high school or college age), it definitely will be inappropriate for you to serve as a surrogate spokesperson for your son with his coach, unless your son requests your assistance. On occasions, a high school-aged player may ask you to talk to his coach. The key point in this situation is to *wait until he does ask, if he does it at all. You should not, under any circumstances, intervene on his behalf unless asked to do so*. A college player will rarely (if ever) ask for your help on his behalf.

Until your son reaches college age, however, it may be necessary for you to intervene with his coach. For example, if all avenues for resolution seem closed and you believe that the coach is endangering the health of his players, you have to be pro-active (e.g., you may have to go to the authorities to address a situation where you feel your son and his teammates may be in physical danger).

Such parental intervention should only be undertaken under extreme circumstances. As your son's mother and advocate, it is imperative that if an abusive environment exists, you must ensure that it is brought to the attention of people or authorities who can address it.

Over the Line

■ *Defining abuse.* Having experienced the various stages of my son's baseball journey, I am far less concerned with verbal abuse than I am with physical abuse. While verbal abuse is bad, if your son has truly learned that baseball is something he does, rather than who he is, he will learn to deal with it. Over time and with maturity, he will develop the ability to discern the difference between what might be genuine, constructive criticism and what is nothing more than mean-spirited, misguided comments.

Physical abuse is another matter, however. It is serious, and it is wrong. When it is occuring, it must be stopped. In that regard, it is important that you are able to recognize the difference between physical toughness and physical abuse. A demanding coach can help your son grow—as an athlete and as a person. A physically abusive coach can harm your son.

Physical abuse can take many forms, for example:

- When a pitcher is required to throw too many pitches in a game or is played in successive games without being given sufficient rest. The numbers on what constitutes too many pitches are somewhat subjective. To a degree, it will vary from athlete to athlete. Eventually, however, a point occurs for all pitchers when enough is enough. (Refer to chapter 13 for an in-depth discussion of this subject.)

- When a coach dismisses a comment made by a player that he is injured or hurt.

- When a coach runs his players until they are so dehydrated that they are placed in physical harm. Even though the number of serious injuries (or even worse, deaths) from such circumstances is extremely rare, even one such incident due to coaching ignorance and insensitivity is one too many.

- When a coach is trying to prove that he (as a coach) can only be successful if his team wins. Such an attitude often comes at the expense of his players' health or dignity.

If any of the following warning signs or behaviors are exhibited by a coach, you should consider taking appropriate action to make sure that his behavior ceases:

- Hitting players
- Using practices to impose punishment
- Over-utilizing pitchers
- Disregarding feedback from a player that he is in physical pain
- Looking the other way if drugs are being used by players
- Taking it too personally if the team loses
- Not allowing parents or other adults to be around during practices

In the aforementioned situation, your first step should be to go to him with your concerns. If, for any reason, this is not a viable option, and if your son is playing in an organized scholastic program (e.g., junior high school or high school), you could consider speaking to the school's athletic director instead. On the other hand, if your son is playing in Little League or is on a traveling team, your most viable option for addressing such circumstances may involve placing your son on a different team. Regardless of the particular situation, however, you should make sure that you discuss your options with your son. Whenever possible, you should include him in the process.

What Not to Do as a Parent

Every situation is unique. The guidelines presented in this book for handling various types of circumstances are simply that, guidelines. It is worth repeating that coaches are often under tremendous pressure. Little League and traveling coaches, for example, are faced with the challenge of dealing with an abundance of unsolicited parental opinion at every turn. Even at the high school level, coaches are being forced more frequently to deal with parental pressure in indirect ways, especially when it involves whether they should hold on to their coaching jobs. Most college coaches don't seem to be bothered too much by parental pressure.

When it comes to speaking to your son's coach, always remember that a silent voice is sweet to hear. There are some things that you should never, as your son's parent, address with his coach. If you truly want to support your son, you must trust your son's ability to make his way. If you struggle with this factor, set aside some time to engage in some activity (e.g., walk, jog, swim, or whatever) that might help clear your head, clarify your thinking, and give a better sense of perspective. If that doesn't help, you might consider sharing your feelings and discussing the issue with someone you trust (e.g., a friend, a fellow baseball mom, a therapist). Be careful not to allow your anguish to reach a point where it negatively affects your life...or your son's. Always remember that some things simply cannot and will not change or are simply outside of your control. Obsessive behavior is usually detrimental to only one person...you.

With regard to interacting with your son's coach, "hush, hush" is the rule for the following topics:

- Your son's playing time
- The position your son should play
- Scheduling of practices, etc.
- Defensive/offensive game strategies
- Appropriate and safe discipline
- Coaching technique and style

While being an advocate for your son is important when it comes to his health and well-being, negotiating with, pressuring, or even bribing your son's coach regarding his playing time is not. In fact, such behavior on your part can impose tremendous pressures and burdens on your son. Regardless of whether your attempts are successful or not, other team members will typically view your son with less respect if you speak with your son's coach about his playing time. It does not matter which parent meddles in such matters. It's still wrong. More often than not, it may be your spouse who takes these issues to your son's coach. Hopefully, if that's the case, you will be able to get your spouse to read this chapter.

Whatever the situation and whatever you do, always remember to keep your son's well-being in mind. Letting your son make his own way is a legacy worth leaving to him.

Reflections

Given the fact that coaches are human beings, it is important to realize that everyone makes mistakes, even diamond moms. On the other hand, it is critical that, to the extent possible, you catch the mistake early, before too much damage is done. Tom House confesses that he and other coaches have done "a pretty good job putting the fire out in a lot of these kids." Great coaches exist, however; you just need to look for them. Focus on those coaches who learn from their mistakes and are advocates for the game, individuals who see the game to be less about them and more about the kids.

In the meantime, don't make excuses or apologize for being and acting like a baseball mom. If circumstances suggest you need to take an action and, for whatever reason, you feel compelled to put on your "Diamond Mom" cap, always remember to wear it with pride…and dignity

8

T-Ball to Travel Ball

Little boys full of big dreams, picking daisies in the outfield.
Hoping the sunbeam shining down will make visible
the road that will lead them to their dreams.

Nothing in the world is cuter than a little five-year-old boy in his first baseball uniform. The hat is almost always oversized, giving the appearance of levitating on his head. His cotton jersey is tucked into his pants and his baseball socks, white and sparkling clean, add to this pristine picture. His shoes are cool—laced and protected by a little black flap. His glove is on one hand, while he punches it with the other hand that holds the magical orb, the baseball. As part of the ritual, he lifts his glove to his nose and breathes in the smell of the leather.

In my mind, there is no better time for the sport than the beginning of the journey. There is something of pure Americana about watching the outfielders who are more interested in picking daisies than catching any ball that *might* happen to be hit toward them. Its simplicity takes us all back to an uncomplicated time, one filled with childlike anticipation of our own future. This is a time of absolute delight for your whole family. You will never forget your son's toothless grin, his awkward play, his naïveté, and the shock on his face when he made his first great play. Relatively speaking, you and your son, at this particular moment in his life, are on an equal playing field. Hopefully, if this period has passed, you have a mental picture album of this time, filled with all the delights of your son's t-ball experiences. Visit it often, especially when you want to recall those delightful moments. It can calm you, transport you back in time to the purity of the sport, and evoke memories of what being a diamond mom can be.

T-ball is a time when many young boys experience the first love of their life. The thief that steals their heart won't be a pigtailed little girl…because boys, at this age anyway, think girls are yucky.

Rather, he will fall in love with the smell of wet dirt, fresh cut grass, and leather gloves. He will fall in love with the thrill of being on a baseball diamond that stirs his heart and calls to his soul. More often than not, his infatuation with the game will be a lifelong love affair, filled with ups and downs. Even when ups and downs occur, the baseball diamond will be the place where he feels at home, where all the troubles of the day are left on the sidelines.

You will recognize your son's passion for the sport immediately. He will spring out of bed on game day, and his uniform will often be on before his eyes are fully open. He will stand in front of a mirror and check out his throwing motion. He will swing an invisible bat at any given moment for no apparent reason. He will feel that practice days are the best days of the week.

If your son loves the game and the idea of playing baseball, it will most likely show up from the time he sets his first step onto the field. On the other hand, if he doesn't like it, no matter how much you encourage or press him to play, he will not. Once he starts his baseball journey, just enjoy the experience until it's over. Eventually, it will end, just as it does for everyone. Keep in mind that even Babe Ruth retired.

Getting Involved

Beyond the love and support you provide your son on his baseball journey, if you have the time, you may decide to devote even more time and energy to the game. There are a number of additional ways that you can contribute to your local baseball community. For example, you could serve as a team mom or even a coach (if you feel you have the knowledge). Another option would be to join the governing board for your son's league. Still another possible way to get more involved in the game would be to serve as a scorekeeper at games.

If you don't know how to be a scorekeeper, many leagues offer classes on how to keep score. If you really want to learn about the game your son is playing, you should volunteer to be the scorekeeper. It is the only way you can be part of the game without ever having played the game. Keeping score offers a perspective that sitting in the stands cannot give you. It is a task that the coach will appreciate. Furthermore, your son will have a sense of gratitude and admiration for the fact that you are trying to understand what he is doing. Keeping score is a great time for you to learn the basics of the game while your son is young. As a rule, the game becomes somewhat more complex as your son's playing career extends over time. As such, knowing the game better and having this foundation can be of great benefit to you.

Another valuable reason to keep score of your son's games is that it gives you a written history of at least part of your son's baseball journey. This history is something your son can share with his children, when he eventually becomes a parent, especially if he has a son or daughter who plays baseball/softball. Personally, I wish I had kept score of my son's games when he played. While I have a book or two of clippings and relevant materials, it is not the same as having a continuous personal record of our time together. Such a record would best be described as *priceless*.

One particular caveat should be emphasized however…knowing about baseball through studying the game is not the same as playing the game. In the same way childless couples cannot really give you insightful advice about raising children, regardless of how many books they have written or read about child rearing, mothers face similar barriers with the game of baseball. You can, however, learn enough about the sport to give your son a healthy respect for your efforts and open up additional avenues of conversation and communication between you.

What's Your League?

Given a choice of leagues in which to play, your son should play for an organized community league that falls under the rules of USA Baseball, the national governing body of amateur baseball. You can access information on USA Baseball at www.usabaseball.com. Be assured if he plays for a league that is under the authority of this governing body that his welfare as a youth baseball player will be protected. At the present time, six leagues adhere to the rules, policies, and procedures of USA Baseball: Amateur Athletic Union, Little League, National High School Coaches Association, Police Athletic League, PONY Baseball, and YMCA. Each of these leagues operates under the general guidelines established by USA Baseball. USA Baseball also oversees training for the U.S. Olympic baseball team. Its sister organization in Canada is Baseball Canada.

Little League

Boys play Little League between the ages of five and 12. Each league is divided into separate divisions by age group: five- and six-year-olds play t-ball; seven- and eight-year-olds play rookie ball; nine- and 10-year-olds play minor ball; and 11- and 12-year-olds play major ball. On occasion, a few gifted 10-year-olds are invited to play in the major division of the league. It should be noted that "t-ball"-level competition is sometimes referred to by other terms, such as "Shetland League," depending on the community or region of the country where this age group plays.

If your son has a talent and/or an affinity for baseball, it will often be evident right from the beginning. Most parents whose sons play collegiate ball or higher report that this is true for their sons. The motor skills involved in playing baseball tend to develop early and appear to be instinctual. More often than not, we take it for granted when our kids are physically gifted and don't even realize how fortunate they are to have such God-given attributes. With regard to his baseball journey, these gifts are a blessing. And if **you,** as his mother, recognize them…well, trust me, his talent will be like a field of flowers to a honeybee on a sunny spring day. Every coach will be looking at him and coveting him for his team.

By the age of 10, if your son has an above-average level of talent, he will receive all kinds of attention. This period is typically a very exciting time for young players and their families. The journey ahead looks exciting, filled with endless possibilities. This is also a time when you will be faced with numerous choices concerning your son. The decisions you make involving your son at this point can influence and impact his life and experiences for years to come.

Community baseball leagues that are affiliated with USA Baseball provide an opportunity for young men to play baseball through their 18th birthday. For those boys who love baseball and do not make their high school teams, it offers a great opportunity for them to continue to play baseball, thereby extending their baseball life.

Travel Teams

If you decide to let your son play on a travel team, such a decision *may* (but not always) cause you (as his parent) to experience conflicts with the individuals who administer community league baseball in your area. If your son chooses to play on a travel team and also wants to participate in community sports, you should be prepared for conflict. Politics normally bloom like weeds in community sports. If your son is above average or stands out, you will probably be faced with potential jealousies, control issues, and irrational thinking that may keep you up nights. If such a situation occurs, you should always remember that your son is in the middle of this conflict and can feel compromised, embarrassed, and resentful if you do not handle it thoughtfully. Exerting your influence in an appropriate manner can help give you perspective.

In these circumstances, it is important that you include your son in the decision-making. Enlisting his input will give him a voice in his own destiny. It will also allow him to learn from this experience, which will help him be better prepared to handle future situations and choices he might encounter. Listen to what he has to say and encourage him to hear your point of view as well. If, after considering all the facts, a decision is made that your son will play both travel and community baseball, you should proceed to the next step.

First, you should communicate with his coaches and let them know what he will be doing. This step is especially critical in the event your son is a pitcher. All coaches love to win. Good coaches know that the primary focus of young teams is the development of the skills and fundamentals that the players will need at later stages of their baseball journey. Furthermore, they realize that while winning is fun and a well-intended goal, it should not be achieved at the cost of any player's physical well-being. Unfortunately, not all coaches subscribe to this philosophy. Certainly, the "winning is everything" crowd doesn't.

Accordingly, it cannot be emphasized enough, you must not, under any circumstances, allow coaches to overuse (i.e., overthrow) your son—especially if he is a pitcher. Above all else, *you must not let your son be dishonest with his travel coach about his playing time away from his travel team. This point is particularly important if your son is a pitcher.*

This is a time when your son is undergoing a period of physical development. His body is growing, and his bones are forming. Misuse will assuredly reduce his future chances of playing. It will simply be a matter of when, not if, he develops an arm, elbow, or back injury. As such, you must not let a momentary, misguided desire on your part gamble away his future opportunities to play baseball. It simply is not worth it.

If your son is a pitcher who is playing on two teams, issues can arise. Accordingly, it is important to be in absolute agreement with the coaches of each of his teams that your son's arm is a priority for them. At the very least, those coaches must be made aware of the fact that it is *your* top priority. If your son is to pitch for one of the teams, he should not be pitching for the other team unless, *and only if*, he has at least four days of rest between the games in which he plays. This stipulation presents a near-impossible scenario and is virtually unrealistic. *The more sensible option for your son in this situation is that he will pitch for one team and play another position for the other team.* (The importance of pitch counts is addressed more thoroughly in Chapter 13.)

In reality, conflict does not always arise when a young athlete attempts to play on two different teams during the same period. Even when it does, the intensity of discord tends to vary from situation to situation. On the other hand, you need to be prepared for the possibility of encountering opposition to your son's wishes, particularly from individuals within your community. Every situation is different. Unfortunately, no single, pat answers exist concerning how to deal with such circumstances. As with all areas of conflict, you should try to approach this situation with dignity, intelligence, and grace, remembering at all times that your son is in the middle of this situation.

Travel ball can (and often does) last through your son's college years. All factors considered, the opportunity for your son to play on travel teams is an honor that can open many doors of opportunity for him. The chance to play with players of similar or better ability will help sharpen his skills, keep him on the edge of his game, and provide him with a comparative basis for determining if he has what it will take to play baseball at the next competitive level.

Once your son begins high school, travel ball teams are relegated to summer play. High school seasons fluctuate from state to state, primarily a by-product of weather-related factors. For the most part, once high school begins, travel or elite teams play only during summer months.

On the Road Again: Tournaments

Tournament play is one of the most memorable aspects of your son playing on elite and travel ball teams. If he plays for a travel team, your son will have the opportunity to journey to other areas to play in baseball tournaments, which involve playing a series of games over a specific period of time, against several teams. As a rule, tournaments are normally scheduled over holiday dates or during summer months.

A Priceless Experience

For boys up to age 12, Cooperstown, New York, offers a journey through "the field of dreams." Cooperstown Dreams Park provides tournament play for boys 12 and under during an 11-week period beginning in mid-June. The week stay offers your family the opportunity to visit baseball's Hall of Fame and experience the charms of this historic region. If your son gets the opportunity to play on a team that participates in this tournament, you should allow him to do so. The boys stay with their coaches in bunkhouses and have the opportunity to experience baseball away from their parents with their buddies, all the while eating, enjoying life, having fun, and making memories. Memories like these, as the saying goes, are priceless.

Things to Take With You to Games

There are certain things that you (as a diamond mom) should take with you to your son's games. Not only will these items help enhance your level of creature comfort, they may be needed by your son at some point either during or after the game, particularly if he is a pitcher.

Warm summer days usually require no more than a soft pad to sit on, sunscreen to protect your skin, a hat to shade your eyes, and a bottle of water. It's also always good to have some aspirin or non-aspirin pain reliever in your purse. Because the weather is sometimes questionable, you may need a few things to help keep you warm (or dry). Furthermore, if your son is a pitcher, you should take a few additional supplies with you to his games. The inventory of materials to consider taking to your son's games should include the following:

- A large soft bag
- A small cooler with ice
- Blankets
- Gloves
- Hats
- Sunscreen (all factors considered, spray is the best option for your son because it will not make his hands greasy)
- Lip balm
- Mosquito repellant (if you live in or visit the mosquito country)
- Pain relievers (aspirin or non-aspirin)
- Water
- Sports drinks
- Snacks for after the game
- Sunflower seeds and/or peanuts (a required food during baseball season)
- A spray bottle if the weather is hot
- Umbrellas for shade or unexpected rain

Extra items for pitchers:

- Plastic bags that zip close and seal tightly
- Plastic sheathing (material that can be used to wrap a bag of ice around your son's arm and shoulder. Plastic can serve as a great makeshift wrap and is actually preferred by most players, because the ice that is enclosed by the wrap surrounds the arm and shoulder or elbow more efficiently.)
- Tiger balm or sports crème (typically applied at home)

You should not let the list overwhelm you. As with all guidelines addressed in this book, you should pick your poison. In fact, on occasion, you may need some additional items that are not on the aforementioned list, for example, food—either for you during the game or for your son after the game. The league your son is playing in may or may not have a snack bar. Travel teams rarely have snack bars unless they are involved in a tournament. Eventually, however, over time you will learn what you need to bring to the games—for you and your son.

Too Much of A Good Thing

All parents want certain things for their kids. They want them to be healthy and active, to use their talents, to stay out of trouble, and to make wise choices. Sometimes, even with all their good intentions, parents are bewildered about their proper role of providing support and love for their children. For example, it is important to really pay attention to your son and his devotion and love for baseball and not confuse his passion for the sport with an over-abundance of activity. In our case, even our son asked for and took a well-deserved break from the game. It did not last for too long, but he took one.

The important point to keep in mind is that if your son comes to you and requests some time off from his sport, you should listen to his request and take him seriously. Far too often, too many talented and gifted players quit the game because they were pressured by their parents to continue playing. Everyone needs a vacation from what they do. If baseball is the path your son is meant to travel, he will return. Space will give your son an opportunity to breathe, a time to reflect. If baseball is the love of his life, he will return to it, renewed, and better for the intermission he has taken from his baseball journey

9

High School

"There is always one moment in childhood when the door opens and lets the future in."

— Deepak Chopra

High school is the point where the rubber meets the road. This is where you, his mother, get completely "off the bus" unless a serious issue occurs regarding his well-being. The term "get off the bus" refers to the fact this is the time for your son to take responsibility for himself. Too many families, ours included, spend too much time trying to encourage (and even sometimes demanding) that their sons practice, work out, or otherwise focus their energy on excelling in the sport they play. It never works. Remember when your son was two or three years old, and he did the "I am a big boy" routine? Well, it's worse now because he can drive…or soon will be able to.

It will not matter what position your son should play. It will not matter whether you think your son is an exceptional athlete. Furthermore, your concern about what your son's coach thinks of him will not be all that important (to anyone but you). What does matter is that your son is aware of his coach's expectations of him…both on and off the field. As a diamond mom, one of your responsibilities will be to help guide (sometimes with actions, rather than words) him through the turmoil he may encounter involving his coaches. It will not be your job, however, to interfere in his conflicts. He must learn to communicate with his coaches if he is to be successful at the next competitive level. Like it or not, disagreements will occur. For instance, you may think that as a freshman, your son has a level of ability that warrants his placement on the varsity team. But either the rules or his coaches say differently. Live with it, because that is all you can do. In other words, simply let go and trust your son's talent.

If you live in a more rural area and your son is an outstanding athlete, high school sports should be an enriching, life expanding experience for him. Residing in an area where baseball is a year-round sport may complicate your son's athletic choices somewhat. An even more potentially confounding factor is if you live in a highly populated area. Our experience occurred in Southern California and involved a high school of 3,400 students, a league considered one of the most difficult in the country, in a county full of baseball talent. Players facing such circumstances have greater challenges when it comes to making the team…and sometimes even greater challenges making the starting lineup once, if and when, they do make a team.

School programs vary from region to region. On the other hand, it does not appear that coaches vary all that much from region to region. You should always keep in mind that coaches are one of the human parts of your son's baseball journey. Your son's high school coach has one primary job to do—win games. He also has to deal with young men at the height of their hormonal development and all the factors that are attendant to transitioning from boyhood to manhood. This period is a time of passage for your son. Whatever struggles or challenges he faces at this point in his life will help him be better prepared to weather his future experiences, particularly if he goes on to play baseball at the collegiate level. In a perfect world, you could wave a magic wand and all coaches would be like John Wooden, the renowned UCLA basketball coach of the 1960s and 1970s. Unfortunately, dreams and wishes don't always come true. John

Wooden was an exceptional coach and even finer person, but his coaching style is not the norm among current coaches (in any sport).

All coaches want to win no matter what level of baseball they coach. High school coaches, however, must work with local talent and play the hand they are dealt with the players from their community. On occasion, a parent may try to change his son's circumstances. For instance, in some highly competitive areas of the country, there are actually parents who will move to a particular community to give their sons an opportunity to play for a highly regarded coach or highly ranked team.

As parents, we all want to do whatever is best for our children. Any opportunity involving our baseball-playing sons is no different. If the situation warrants it, those circumstances may include supporting our son's decision to play on a particular team. With regard to our actions, however, it is important to note that a fine line exists between reason and insanity—a line many of us have crossed on occasion. The key is to spend more time on the reasoned side of the line than on the insane side, a task made even more difficult by baseball's ever-evolving nature. In reality, all is not fair in baseball, as it allegedly is in love and war.

My son's high school years were a very difficult time for me because I was someone who knew little about the process he was going through as an athlete. On one hand, I wanted to make it perfect for him. On the other hand, my inability to do that nearly drove me crazy until his senior year when I finally realized that there was very little I could do to change his experience in a meaningful way. I had to step back and reevaluate myself. Fortunately, I discovered a few small, yet significant, areas existed in which I could still have influence on my son's baseball journey. The same holds true for all diamond moms. By focusing on what you *can* do and, if this connection emanates on your part from strength and confidence rather than from fear or anger, your involvement as a baseball mom will be much more meaningful and enjoyable—no matter what level with which you are dealing. Taking a reasoned, levelheaded approach to your son's baseball experience can help him immensely, although you might actually benefit more than he does if you do.

Academic Challenges

Our country is fortunate to have a public education system in which everyone has the opportunity to learn. Since the vast array of schools that dot the educational landscape in the United States feature a variety of learning styles and approaches, each situation needs to be evaluated individually. As a parent, one of your challenges is to take advantage of programs that will help your son be successful and that may address his unique learning needs and interests. In that regard, one step you can take is to call your son's school and find out if it offers any programs, clubs, or activities that will help prepare him for life after high school, particularly if he intends on going onto college. School is and should always be your first concern for your son.

Research shows that many athletes suffer from mild-to-extreme learning difficulties. In that regard, you may face another critical challenge as a parent; specifically, the need to acknowledge his challenge. Addressing a learning disability as early as possible is important in order to help your son successfully pursue his post-high school interests. If your son suffers from a learning disability, you should get it diagnosed and chronicled early. If he has a learning disability and you have not officially documented it prior to high school, you should do so *immediately*. Pretending it does not exist can only place undue pressure on your son and can create a feeling that his learning limitation/disability is somehow a personal flaw, rather than being just simply what it is—a physical, biological condition.

If your son has a learning disability, you should talk to him about his particular challenge and help him understand and be at peace with his circumstances. If he has dyslexia or other reading disabilities, nothing can be done to eliminate this neurological disorder. On the other hand, proven programs and trained professionals exist who can help provide the guidance that will enable him to effectively manage his disability to the degree he is able. Being a positive and cooperative advocate for him in this issue may be the most important steps you can take to help him. It is also a powerful demonstration of your love for him and your belief in him as a human being. Teaching him to work *with* the system of public education can translate into other areas of his life as he matures and grows.

On the Team

From the beginning and throughout the duration of his days as a high school baseball player, your son will face a need to balance the academic, social, and baseball demands on his life. Depending on the program, baseball may even be a year-round sport for him. The dedication demanded of him during this time will test you and him. One factor that may affect how he holds up to these demands is what type of individual he is. As a rule, there are two kinds of players who will make the high school baseball team: "developing" and "mature" athletes.

The mature player was probably born this way, seeming like an "old soul" from the moment you held him in your arms. He is a good student, involved in extracurricular activities, such as student government, and may even hold down a part-time job. He almost always puts his responsibilities involving home, school, and his baseball workout ahead of his friends, his girlfriend, and/or his social calendar. He exhibits discipline, both on and off the field. Coaches love this type of individual. College coaches and scouts drool after these young men. They are, quite frankly, somewhat of an enigma.

The "developing" player is where (dare it be said) 98 percent of the boys tend to find themselves. During their first three years of high school ball they are striving and working hard to make their mark and be noticed for the opportunity to play for a college or possibly be drafted. Beyond that scenario, however, they are also taking the time to enjoy their friends, high school, girls, movies, and whatever else falls in their path along the way. All factors considered, if they are making their grades and being responsible, respectful young adults, both tracks can co-exist peacefully.

It is essential that you are comfortable with the category in which your son falls. Knowing who your son is and being honest with yourself about his type of personality and his level of commitment to his sport can help you create clear and concise boundaries concerning his actions. You should communicate openly with him about his choices. It is as important for your son to have guidelines regarding what you require of him, as it is for you to have a road map on a car trip. Knowing where you are starting your journey from is equally as important as knowing where you want to go. Furthermore, you will have a hard time arriving at your intended destination if you don't know what roads to take to get there. The point is that your son will feel more self-assured about his present *and* his future if he knows his boundaries and what is required of him.

Like it or not, you can no more turn your "developing" player into a "mature" player at this stage than you can change a piece of coal into a diamond. Any change (if possible) can take time. If your son is a diamond, life will soon enough morph him into his own unique gem. Until then, when dealing with your son, you should always be firm, disciplined, and, above all else, loving. At no time should you let him get away with being anything less than he can be.

Social Calendars and Girlfriends

High school can be a challenging period for parents, especially if your son wants to go on to college and continue playing baseball. The time demands that your son may encounter during this phase of his baseball journey will typically require a great deal of discipline on his part to prioritize them, but how he does will help set the precedent for college.

You should clearly inform your son of your family's rules and requirements, all the while making sure that he understands clearly what *your* expectations are and what *his* should be if he wants to go on to play at the next competitive level. Even if the next level involves attending a community college (as opposed to a four-year institution), he will still need to be disciplined and have an appropriately balanced life. Frequently, the rigors and demands of making a higher commitment will discourage individuals from putting in the effort required to fulfill that commitment. If the vision you have for your son does not match your son's personal vision he holds for himself, then it is important to stop and ask yourself some very important questions. Do you honestly believe you can entice, bribe, insist, coerce, demand or shape your son's vision into the one held by you or his father? It can be liberating, as parents, to acknowledge and accept that we can no more decide for *our* children than our parents could decide for *us*. It is far better for you to be honest with yourself now, than to expend your emotions and resources on a vision that you hold that may be diametrically opposed to the image your son holds for himself.

Socially, your son may be popular (as many athletes are) and may want to attend all the dances, events, and the extracurricular activities that he can, especially during his senior year. My son was always told that he would receive the degree of freedom that he earned, based upon the guidelines that we set forth for the family. The key point is that you should be aware that you might have to deal with popularity issues and social circumstances, especially if your son is an extroverted, people person. No one is recommending that you should "give in" to your son's wishes and whims. Rather, you should try to guide him into making decisions that will support his future, however he sees it unfolding. One of the saddest steps in the maturation process is to look back with regret at what we didn't do and should have. To a degree, our experience and accumulated knowledge can serve as the binoculars to the future for our sons.

Playing Multiple Sports

Your son's ability to play different sports during the school year will depend on several factors, including the structure of sports programs at the high school he attends, his level of interests and skills, and his personal dedication to the sports he wants to play. Not surprising, this issue is one that often inspires debate and controversy.

In reality, some baseball players are simply good athletes and are able to play multiple sports, while keeping up with the academic rigors that are attendant to that situation. On the other hand, sports often overlap each other, thereby creating conflicts with coaches and players. Furthermore, your son will face different training requirements for different sports. To a degree, conditioning for baseball involves somewhat different requirements than other sports do. As such, if your son plays multiple sports, you should consider meeting with his coaches to help ensure that whatever conditioning regimen he is required to perform (over the course of the various seasons) is appropriate for his capabilities and needs.

A benefit exists for your son to play multiple sports. Activity-wise, it keeps your son involved. It also can enhance or help him maintain his level of physical conditioning, assuming his sport-specific workout requirements are sound and coordinated. If your son can and wants to play several sports in the same year, you should support and encourage him. On one hand, it's his life to lead, and he will only have one opportunity to be a high school student. For another, if he wants to play college baseball, colleges love a multiple-sport athlete because it shows discipline in character…not to mention talent. The recurring point that must be emphasized is that whatever sport your son chooses to participate in, it must be something he wants to do.

The Real Deal

In a perfect world, life would be fair, and baseball would always be measured by productivity and performance. It would be nice to live in a world where it didn't matter what we looked like, whom we knew, or who our parents are. Baseball, however, is real life, only magnified. Not because baseball is something that is more important than life, but because, in a very real sense, it is life. Furthermore, life, in words that have filtered down from generation to generation, is not always fair.

That simple reality is exemplified by the fact that sometimes talented baseball players are overlooked by coaches. The following story illustrates the point. I once interviewed a parent who had a son with a lot of ability as a baseball player. This young man had entered high school and had had an outstanding year as a freshman player. Not only was he a capable utility man (i.e., he was able to play almost any position), he ended his freshman year with one of the highest batting averages on the team. The following year, he was cut from the baseball program.

He was devastated. He talked to the coaches. His parents talked to the coaches. Nevertheless, he remained "cut" and took a year off from baseball. He never stopped loving the game, however. While he questioned the reasons for being cut, he eventually accepted his circumstances.

One of the most amazing factors about this boy is that he did not give up. He tried out for the team again during his junior year and made the team and then continued to play throughout his senior year. Not only did he return, he became a team leader and was honored at the end of his senior year as one of the top 20 baseball players in the state. He now plays for a Division I college program.

The real value in this young man's story is that on occasion, good players get cut from their teams. The key point is that no player (or his family) should let someone else define who he is. The question is not whether we fail to "make it," but whether we fail to try. One minor bit of information you may or may not know that may help clarify this issue…Michael Jordan was cut from his high school basketball team.

10

Recruiting and Scout Process

"[Doors are] holes in walls that offer us a way out or a way in. Just putting your hand on the knob and seeing if it turns can make you weak in the knees."

— Mark D. Sanders and Tia Sillers,
I Hope You Dance

If you read Webster's dictionary carefully, you will discover that "recruit" is a noun, as well as a verb. It is an important detail to remember if your son is fortunate enough to reach a point in his baseball journey where he is recruited.

Recruiting is a business and, like any business, it is not personal. If you want to maintain your sanity during the process when your son is being recruited, you should try to equate the scenario to shopping for something you want to buy. Your son will be considered a commodity—part of the ongoing supply of "new" players to replenish the team. The term "new" is applicable because your son will be a visitor to the team that recruits him until he proves himself, which will be his job…in the business of baseball.

No one has ever reasonably claimed that achieving your dream is a cakewalk. Even if your son is being considered or has dreams of one day playing professional baseball, he still has to face the fact that baseball is a job. In order for him to be taken seriously for this "job," he must consistently play well. He must work to improve his already exceptional skill level. He must commit and fully focus on the task at hand. All of these steps are necessary if his dream is to become a reality.

In my mind, baseball will always be a lovely, magical game. For the most part, most players who go professional appear to still feel that way about the game. On the other hand, most fairy tales also have their practical, realistic side. Like almost everything worth having (e.g., marriage), baseball, at the professional level, is work. And like marriage, when two people in a partnership understand the reality that comes with romance, it can be a wonderful, life-fulfilling experience.

The primary focus of this chapter is to familiarize you with the process, procedures, and potential pitfalls involved in recruiting. If you'd like to obtain additional information on recruiting, you have options. For example, for a step-by-step manual on the recruiting process, you may want to consider purchasing *Recruiting Realities* by Jack Renkens (www.recruitingrealities.com). Its "workbook" design is very user friendly and provides detailed instruction for families and athletes. The material contained within its pages is useful, enlightening, and time proven. On the other hand, if you prefer to take a more personal approach in your search for information, you can contact Renkins' company by telephone at 800-242-0165.

So, how does the recruiting process work?

The NCAA and Your Son

The National Collegiate Athletic Association (NCAA) is the organization that oversees and implements rules and regulations as they apply to student-athletes who attend four-year NCAA member college institutions. The NCAA is the ruling body designed to protect student-athletes who are college bound, as well as those student-athletes attending and playing for member colleges. It is the single most important organization in your son's life if he is planning on attending a NCAA school. Accordingly, you and your son should become familiar with the rules of the NCAA as he prepares to play baseball at the college level. In that regard, you are encouraged to visit the organization's web site at www.ncaa.org or write or call the NCAA (700 W. Washington St., PO Box 6222, Indianapolis, IN 46206-6222; (317) 917-6222) and request that information be sent to you. It is important to seek out any information that can help your son prepare for the next step in his baseball journey.

The NCAA governs and regulates the recruiting process for your son. It publishes a manual, *The NCAA Handbook*, which includes over 400 pages that outline the rules and regulations that can affect your student-athlete. Specific guidelines regarding recruiting can be found in the Handbook, beginning at Section 13.1. NCAA policies cover issues such as minimum grade requirements, athlete discipline, drug abuse regulations (including lists of prohibited drugs and consequences of use), and enrollment…to name just a few. The NCAA also sets rules regarding school transfers and the number of years of playing eligibility a player will have.

It is important to note that college recruiters are not allowed to contact you or your son *prior* to July 1, following his junior year of high school. Recruiters are allowed to make one visit in April of the athlete's junior year—an event that must occur on the athlete's high school campus. This visit is subject to applicable recruiting-calendar restrictions.

One of the most important things to know about the NCAA is that your son must apply to the NCAA Clearinghouse to establish his eligibility and must meet his eligibility requirements to play at a designated NCAA college. High school counselors can help you with this process. You can access information regarding your son's application to the NCAA Clearinghouse at www.ncaaclearinghouse.net. Once the NCAA deems him academically eligible, he will be assigned a personal ID number to use when applying to colleges. You can also obtain information about registering your son with the NCAA by contacting the NCAA Clearinghouse either in writing or by telephone (301 ACT Drive, Box 4043, Iowa City, IA, 52243-4043; (877) 262-1492).

The National Association of Intercollegiate Athletes

The NAIA is another well-respected association that governs student-athletes. Established in 1937, The NAIA currently oversees almost 300 colleges across the United States. While the NAIA includes a few larger colleges as members, most of its members are smaller, private colleges. If your son is considering attending a NAIA college, you can obtain more information at www.naia.org. The NAIA's address and telephone number are 23500 W. 105th St., Olathe, KS, 66051; and (913) 791-0044, respectively.

The role of the NAIA is similar to the NCAA, but distinct differences exist between the two organizations. As your son heads for college, you will want to make yourself familiar with the student-athlete requirements for each group. The NAIA's web site is very user-friendly. On the right side of the first page to appear is a heading entitled "Information" with a subheading entitled "Student-Athlete Information." The available information is printer-friendly as well.

Who Does What?

For the sake of clarity (and not necessarily by definition), "recruiters" are defined in this chapter as men who scout for colleges, while "scouts" are referred to as men who work for professional teams. (Sorry, ladies. Personally, I have never seen a female scout or recruiter at any baseball game I've ever attended.)

College Recruiters

Most college recruiters are generally an assistant coach (often the pitching coach) who scouts for his college's program. Even though college recruiters cannot speak to any player directly until July 1 following the athlete's junior year, many of the college recruiters identify the names of players in whom they're interested much earlier. It is within the scope of the NCAA rules for coaches to "advertise" their program through e-mails sent to athletes in a newsletter format, looking to grab the interest of these individuals prior to July 1. College recruiters recruit athletes from both high schools and community colleges. NCAA rules slightly vary between high school and community college players regarding how they should be treated and/or can be approached.

Generally speaking, if your son has sufficient talent, he will be discovered. Keeping his talent a secret is a bit like hiding a candle under a bushel of straw. If he has above average talent and plays for a team with no superstars who draw recruiters and scouts, you should take under consideration the advice presented in this chapter in the section, "What You Can Do."

The July 1 personal contact restriction can place enormous mental and emotional pressure on your son. If he has aspirations of playing college baseball, he will be hoping for calls from colleges on that date. Accordingly, as a parent, you should be sensitive to his anxiety. His concern can manifest itself in a number of fashions, including being disguised as forgetfulness, silence, tentativeness, or in a million other ways. As such, you should be patient with your son during this period. It can be a very scary time for him, especially if his expectations are high.

A number of factors can influence whether your son receives a call from an interested college recruiter. While talent always plays a role in the decision concerning when and if such a call will be made, the grades of the athlete, how many kids a school is trying to recruit, and what positions the school is attempting to fill (and whether your son plays one of those positions) can also be determinants. Furthermore, July 1 is not the only time colleges can call. Recruiting calls are made throughout the academic year. In reality, if your son has talent, he will eventually be contacted by a school.

Professional Scouts

Major league teams carry 15 or so professional scouts on their payroll who travel and watch baseball games throughout the United States. These scouts are assigned by area and attend games in search of promising and talented players. They also follow travel teams,[1] scout leagues,[2] and attend showcases.[3] Major leagues also utilize the services of freelance, commissioned scouts who operate independently. All factors considered, scouts work and travel tirelessly, spending countless hours and days on the road during baseball season. Even in the best of circumstances, it's a tough life.

Guidelines for Recruiters and Scouts

College recruiters are allowed to approach both high school and community college players under very strict guidelines that are outlined in detail by the NCAA and the NAIA. *Professional scouts*, on the other hand, are subject to similar standards of the NCAA and the NAIA, but are also guided by rules set forth by the commissioner of professional baseball. As a rule, *professional scouts* have far more flexibility regarding time lines and frequency of contacts when performing their duties than do *college recruiters.*

If a team has a high-profile player, as many as 30-to-40 recruiters/scouts may be in attendance at a high school or college game. If the player being scouted is a pitcher, the scene is like a modern version of the wild, wild west. Each scout has his speedgun ready and aimed, once the pitcher sets to throw a pitch. Watching the rites and rituals associated with recruiting and scouting can be almost as entertaining as the game itself.

The process can also be intimidating for players. For example, the scenario can be frightening when as many as 20 scouts are surrounding a bullpen, while pointing speedguns at a senior high school pitcher who is warming up for a game—a big game that is occurring, more often than not, at the end of his high school season. Even though the player may look cool and collected on the outside, his insides are being

---

1. Travel teams are baseball squads whose rosters typically feature the elite players in your area. With independent (usually volunteer) coaches, these teams are generally part of a travel team league, which is a league that is specifically designed to provide an opportunity for player development. Travel team seasons are usually held during either the summer or fall. A few winter leagues are conducted in the Sun Belt region.

2. Scout leagues are leagues created by professional scouts that allow players to showcase their talent for colleges and other professional scouts. Scout baseball teams are generally found in the Sun Belt areas, such as Northern and Southern California, Texas, Arizona, and Florida. Your son can try out for a scout team, but more often than not, he will be invited to play by the representative scout/coach. If referred, he must still be selected by the coach to play for the team. If you live in one of the Sun Belt areas and want to find a scout team for your son, you should contact the corporate office of the major league team nearest you and ask for information.

3. Showcases are events put on by organizations to allow players to demonstrate their playing ability. They are designed specifically for the purpose of providing scouts and recruiters with a centralized area in which to view players.

assaulted by a barrage of emotions. On one hand, this experience can be quite exhilarating for him. On the other hand, all that is running through his mind is, "throw harder, throw harder, the scouts are watching, the scouts are watching..."

In summary, the college recruiting process truly begins in your son's junior year. Some players decide to sign early with the college of their choice (in November of their senior year), while others wait until the spring of their senior year or the summer following it.

Likely Candidates

■ *High-profile players*. These players represent only two percent of the player population. You will find them nationally ranked and listed in leading magazines, such as *Baseball America*. As a rule, players may appear on one or both of the listings. One list identifies the top-ranked players who are eligible for the major league draft, while another list sets forth the top high school and Division I, II, and IIII college players in the country.

■ *Good/outstanding players*. Another possible scenario involves a situation where your son may be a talented baseball player who is not nationally ranked, but is being (or could be) considered by colleges for their diamond programs. In fact, over 70,000 to 80,000 young men play collegiate baseball each year. There is always a place for a good, above-average athlete/baseball player on a college team somewhere in America. While colleges will always try to find good players, it is also a good idea for your son to do his own research and identify colleges with baseball programs that fit him not only athletically, but academically as well.

Things Scouts/Recruiters Look for in Players

Many of the points discussed in this section were addressed earlier in the book, but are worth repeating, especially because they come from the "horse's mouth." For example, Craig Weissman, a professional scout for the Florida Devil Rays organization, once responded to a question from me that he thought that the following attributes are important in the execution of his role as a scout. *"Scouts look first to the player's talent—what they can see with the naked eye. Next, we look for intangibles, such as hustle and passion for the game. After talent and the intangibles, we look to see what kind of aptitude and savvy the player has. Is he intelligent on the field, is he fluid, does he have confidence in himself and his ability, and is he athletic? When we look at a pitcher, we look to his pitch speed, his command on the mound, his balance, and his sense of rhythm. All players are measured for their athleticism, strength, flexibility, foot speed, accuracy, and quickness."*

In that same vein, Tony Gwynn, head baseball coach at San Diego State University, once told me: *"I look for players who not only love the game, but have passion for it as well. Loving a sport and having passion to play the sport are different in my eyes. Loving comes and goes, but passion stays forever. I feel a player needs passion to survive the inevitable struggles that come with the sport. If your son loves baseball, feed his passion by not being overly concerned or emotional about his success…at least not in front of him. The true heroes in life really never give up; they just learn something from their setbacks."*

Most scouts and recruiters look not only at a player's current ability, but also at his potential. Is the player still growing and maturing, or has he reached his full height and strength? Some young men will continue to grow into their 20s, while others reach their full height and maturity much earlier. Recruiters and scouts will look to see and notice certain telling factors, for example, if your son is in shape, how he manages himself on the field—with coaches, umpires, and other players, and how he manages stress.

You may be wondering what, if anything, you can do, as a mother, to help your son with the attributes for which scouts and recruiters are looking. In reality, you can do nothing about his talent or what he does with it. What you can do is be honest with him, let him to know that he is responsible for his own life, and be there when he needs your love and assistance. In the end, that is all you can ever do as a parent. One thing you absolutely should not do to help your son is to "sell" or "oversell" your son to the scouts. It is the scouts' job to seek out the cream of the crop—and as the saying goes, cream will rise by itself. If you try to "sell" your son, you may end up placing tremendous unnecessary pressure on him. When it comes to professional scouts, the Beatles had it right—"let it be."

All factors considered, becoming a professional baseball player takes stamina, guts, and hard work. Players have to have all that and then more if their dreams to play professional baseball one day are to become a reality. They must prove themselves over and over again. Scouts and coaches are almost unanimous in their opinion on the inevitability of opportunity: "If a player has talent and develops himself, he will get noticed eventually."

Preparing Your Son for College Recruiting

As his mother, you can take a number of steps to help enhance your son's chances of being recruited by a college, including the following:

■ *Documentation.* With the exception of looking back at your son's fondest childhood memories, documenting his baseball accomplishments prior to high school is strictly an exercise of the heart. The memories you collect may be worth their weight in gold to you, but they have absolutely no impact on his marketability as a college player. The reason is quite simple. As a young athlete, your son has a maturing and physically developing body. A boy of 12 years who is two heads taller than his friends may be of average-to-below-average height as a 14- or 16-year-old. As a rule, his physiological development from ages 14 to 17 is not usually as visibly apparent as it is from ages two to five. On the other hand, the physical differences that occur during this later period are far more significant.

Once your son reaches his sophomore year of high school, you may want to keep track of any available materials relevant to his baseball journey, including newspaper clippings about him, any awards he receives, pictures (both moving and still) of live play, and his on-the-field statistics. Subsequently, you can incorporate any of the key points in the materials you gathered in an athletic resume for him The resume should emphasize his strong points (e.g., if he is a pitcher, his ball-to-strike ratio, or if he is an infielder, his fielding percentage) and his obvious strengths (e.g., batting average, ERA, on-base percentage, pitch speed, types of pitches, etc.).

■ *Resumes.* As was previously mentioned, should your son be in the top tier of the player population, the scouts will find him. On the other hand, if your son is an above-average player, but not as visible as a top-level player, he may need to be proactive in his efforts to help the college of his choice notice him. In that regard, preparing and utilizing a resume may be helpful. The rules allow him to forward resumes to the colleges of his choice beginning in his junior year. Being visible and keeping the coaching staff up to date on his development as a player can help him be considered for the college of choice.

Two schools of thought exist on the subject of whether athletic resumes have meaningful value. Some coaches disregard resumes, especially ones that are mailed through national scouting agencies. Other coaches appreciate not having to do all the legwork themselves. The best way to know how the college of his choice wants the issue handled is to have your son telephone the staff at that school and simply ask if they accept information from college-bound student athletes. If your family has the resources and means, you can create your own personal resume and letter, which can be, on occasion, a far less expensive, more effective approach.[4]

As you prepare your son's resume, it is important that you do not inflate his ability or exaggerate his accomplishments. The truth is relatively easy to discover, and if you have inflated the facts concerning his baseball skills, not only can you interfere with his ability to get into the program he wants to join, you will also have forever compromised his integrity. Rumor has it that a player's reputation travels through the baseball grapevine faster than wild fires through a dry forest.

■ *Academics.* Another step you can take to help your son do all that he can to be recruited by a college is to encourage him to stay on track scholastically, and to get

4. A sample letter can be found in the Appendix of this book.

tutors and extra help if and when he needs them. *While it may be in your son's mind he is going to college to play baseball, the truth is that he gets to play baseball only if he gets into college.* While the NCAA requires an athlete to have a 2.0 grade-point average to be eligible to play athletics, a grade average that low will not be helpful in his efforts to be admitted to most four-year, NCAA colleges. In fact, the opposite is true; it will be an impediment. In order for your son to be considered seriously for any college, he will need to carry at least a 2.6 grade-point average. In reality, if he wants his academic record to be a meaningful asset, he should have at least a 3.0 (on a 4.0 scale) average.

Grades can be a significant factor in whether many athletes will play past high school. One of the mothers I had the opportunity to interview shared a story with me that reinforced this point. It is particularly relevant if your son regards school as a necessary evil and does not take his grades seriously.

As her story goes, her son, who was struggling academically, received a telephone call at home one evening from a former high school counselor who had been following his exploits as a baseball player. The student-athlete was an outstanding player, but his grades were lagging. Knowing how much this student-athlete loved baseball and knowing what kinds of grades it would take for him to have the opportunity to play at the college level, the counselor told him, "Your senior year should not be the highlight of your life." In reality, the counselor's message should also apply to community college and college…and perhaps to life in general. The key to a life well-lived is to make every day count. In other words, "do your best and leave the rest." Everything will work out.

Being Proactive

■ *Shopping for a college.* Even though colleges cannot contact your son until after July 1 following his junior year, you can encourage him to begin the process of identifying colleges in which he might be interested as early as his sophomore year. One factor that should influence his efforts in this regard is to consider colleges that match his academic interests. If, for example, he has expressed a desire to study literature in college, he should not waste his time looking at a school that offers a curriculum that focuses on science. Although such an admonition can seem very logical, this point can be missed if your son is enamored with the baseball program of a particular college. In order for your son's college experience to be a good fit for him and his future, it is essential that athletic endeavors and his academic interests compliment each other.

Depending on the situation, several other factors may need to be considered when determining where your son might go to college, including his age and his comfort level in being away from home. Indirect costs can also be a consideration. For example, a school that is too far away from your home can become a relatively expensive proposition if he needs/wants to come home for any reason other than for the holidays.

■ *Contacting college coaches*. Getting in touch with the coaching staff at a school in which he is interested is your son's job. *You should absolutely not contact the colleges for him*. Once he has determined which colleges and baseball programs best fit his needs, he can forward information to the coach or recruiting coach via e-mail or through snail mail. He is not subject to any restrictions regarding how often he contacts a school or what he communicates to college coaches. *How* he approaches this task is the primary issue. Always being mindful of acting respectfully and exhibiting good manners, your son can consider the following steps in this regard:

- Select schools that offer a curriculum that matches his academic interests and then narrow that list down to those schools that can meet both his academic and his baseball aspirations.

- Contact the schools in which he is interested to determine which coach at a particular institution is responsible for recruiting and whether he accepts individual letters and/or resumes from prospects.

- Get the name and the proper spelling, an e-mail address, and/or mailing address for each coach who is to be contacted.

- Send personal information to each coach.

- Periodically update each coach on his personal progress.

When someone once said that baseball is a business, they were not kidding. Unless your son is a widely regarded player, it is his responsibility to market his talent. While he may not feel comfortable undertaking such a role, it is just one more step on his road to his maturity. In all likelihood, he will need your help. On the other hand, it must be his voice that any coach hears. It is also important for him to know that not only will he be promoting his skills as a baseball player; he will be marketing himself as a young man. As is true in almost all sales, personal relationships are everything. If his talent merits consideration by a particular college, the more he can develop a personal relationship with the schools in which he is interested, the better chance he has of being accepted into their programs.

■ *An important point*. One of the more lamentable stories I heard when I was researching this book involved a Division I head coach. The coach was seriously looking at a player and was considering offering the player a full ride to the school. The family had traveled to the college and was returning from lunch when the mother suggested something to her son. Her son responded to her in an insulting, disrespectful way. The coach made an immediate decision to withdraw his offer. He assumed if the player spoke that way to his mother, he would one day speak to him in the same way. The player lost his chance to play for this talented coach, lost his opportunity to attend college at a high-level academic institution, and ended up accepting a scholarship offer to play baseball at a school he eventually left before graduating.

Delicate Dilemma

No easy answer exists to the question of whether your son should go to college or play professional baseball upon graduation from high school. When addressing this issue, the circumstances should be weighed by your family, especially by your son. This issue is a matter you can explore and discuss with your son, but it is not a question you can answer for him.

Geoff Miller of *Winning Mind* has conducted research that focused on how players decided between attending college and choosing a professional baseball career immediately out of high school. The results of his study indicated that players who came from families that valued education tended to choose college, even though they were not pressured to do so by their parents. In most of the cases he looked at, the players told him that their parents allowed them to make their own decisions.

Parents struggle every day with letting go. I once remember having conversations with friends on this issue. To my shock and utter dismay, I had morphed into my parents. After all, in my mind, I had experience and knowledge and answers to the most simple of life's questions. Even something as elementary as my son carrying an umbrella to school when it was raining became a critical concern for me. Fortunately, a dear and kind friend counseled me, "What will happen if your son gets wet?" With a tone of self-righteous indignation, I responded, "Well, how about colds, flu, missed school…" Then, she asked me the most important question of all: "Are you willing to walk with your kids every day and carry the umbrella?" It was plainly evident to me that I did not want that job. Of course, my reply was an emphatic "no."

One of the hardest things parents have to do in life is to let their children make their own decisions, especially ones that from the parent's point of view are life changing. Understandably, choosing a life path is a far more important question than whether or not to carry an umbrella. Such a decision on your part brings up a far more important question: "Do you trust your son to handle his own life?"

Deciding whether to go to college or play professional baseball is an issue in which you must allow your son room to find his own answers. You can be there for him, listen to his concerns, and even share your concerns with him, but in the end, the decision must be his, because he will have to live with it. He will have to wake up to it every day. He will have to put in the time and effort to make it work (whatever his choice). His willingness to confront life's challenges and his ability to accept whatever life throws his way will be enhanced if he is the one deciding his fate.

In reality, no magic formula exists for the "right" way to answer the question of what your son should do after his high school days have ended, because each person and every situation are unique. Hopefully, you have done all the things you needed to do to get him to this point in his life's journey. Accordingly, you need to trust that whatever you have given him is strong enough to enable him to make the "right" decision for *him*, whatever that decision might be. Not only will your faith and trust in him strengthen your relationship with him, it will also enhance his efforts to become a self-assured adult.

11

College and Beyond

"Education is learning what you didn't even know you didn't know."

— Daniel J. Boorstin

Sending your son off to college can feel like you are setting a kite loose in the wind. Even if you have string attached to the kite, once the kite catches the wind, it will toss and turn with little regard for the string that tries to keep it grounded. Like the kite up in the wind drift, your son's freshman year of college is most likely his first taste of freedom, and sometimes the wind can be elusive. It can also be bittersweet for moms. It is a scary time as we face a situation where our sons are making decisions away from our watchful eye. Their freedom creates a scenario where it feels like we are losing control—a circumstance that can leave us frustrated and liberated at the same time.

For our sons, this period is a thrilling time. Little do they know that it is a time for "fast-track maturity." On occasion, they will experience excitement, a boundless sense of energy, and an optimistic zest for life; at other times, however, they will feel overwhelmed, afraid, intimidated, and frustrated. More often than not, they will bounce back and forth between those conflicting emotions, somewhat like a ping-pong ball.

Scholarships and Baseball

The NCAA governs the distribution of scholarships by college athletic programs. Concerning the scholarship program effort in the United States, the NCAA manual states:

> Athletic scholarships for undergraduate student-athletes at Division I and Division II schools are partially funded through the NCAA membership revenue distribution. About $1 billion in athletic scholarships are awarded each year. Over 126,000 student-athletes receive either a partial or full athletic scholarship. However, these scholarships are awarded and administered directly by each academic institution, not the NCAA. Division III schools offer only academic scholarships. They do not offer athletic scholarships.

Of that $1 billion pool, football programs receive a majority of the scholarship funding (as many as 90 full-time scholarships per Division I school), followed by basketball. Many football sports programs generate a tremendous revenue stream for their colleges, which is why they tend to receive a greater piece of the scholarship pie.

Baseball is a quite different story, however. When the dust settles, college baseball programs are only given, on average, a total of 11.7 scholarships per school, which when awarded, must be distributed among as many as 25 players on a team's spring roster. Colleges give different degrees of baseball scholarships. Some schools provide partial scholarships to a number of individuals fortunate enough to be given them, while others may opt to give one or two players full scholarships, and then divide whatever scholarship funds are left among the remaining players. Furthermore, once scholarships are given, individual baseball programs will treat how they are dealt with differently. Some schools will pull a scholarship if the player does not perform or meet the expectations of the coaching staff. Other college baseball programs have a rule that once the scholarship is given, it belongs to the player until he graduates, quits the team, or transfers from the school. With only 11.7 baseball scholarships available to as many as 25 players, the challenges that programs and players face are all too obvious.

The Romance

Remember when you and your husband or partner dated? His clothes were always neat, and his shirt was tucked in. He always smelled good and was clean-shaven. Rarely did he show a fit of temper, and never, ever, did he belch in front of you. His demands of you were rare. On occasion, he may have even opened the car door for you. Every once in awhile, he gave you flowers, perhaps for no other reason than he was thinking of you. During this courting ritual, he might have even surprised you by planning a getaway trip to a bed and breakfast or a sunlit resort over a long weekend. On your birthday, he might have cooked your favorite meal for you. He always listened quietly to your concerns, all the while smiling and nodding his head in understanding when you spoke to him. At some point, there was a glow, a moment in all the romance when you fell in love with him, and you knew you were ready to make a commitment to a relationship with him.

Once you made a commitment, you got married or moved in together. Then, reality set in. You discovered his eccentricities, and he discovered yours. In other words, you became a couple. Trash needed to be taken out and bills needed to be paid. Conflicts arose; demands reared their not-so-attractive head. And so on, ad nauseum. Recruiting is the same romantic dance. Once your son is "married" to the institution, the romance ends, and it ends abruptly.

College recruiters will do and say and be as charming and charismatic as an impassioned lover. It is even worse than courting and marriage, because in order for the romance to take off *and continue*, the player has to perform and deliver. At the college level, baseball is a job. Players tend to survive the demands and challenges inherent in this job, because they are in love with it and have a passion for it. It is not, however, an "until-death-do-us-part" arrangement.

The point is not that coaches are dishonest. Rather, during the recruiting process, they are trying to make their program as attractive as possible to you and your son. Far too often, they will entice your son with all kinds of promises that do not always materialize, especially if they are not offering your son scholarship money. If scholarship money is offered, they tend to put a little more effort into the player to assure his success. If no money has been given to your son and your son is being recruited as a walk-on, he must be prepared to make his presence felt. He will need to work harder than anyone else, stand out above everyone else, and excel past everyone else to become a visible, viable member of the team (and be treated accordingly).

Not surprisingly, one of the primary focuses of college coaches is to win games to keep their jobs. Winning games, however, is not always enough. They must also have winning seasons and make their school attractive to players, sponsors, and alumni. To a great degree, winning games is a direct by-product by which coaches select players for their teams. If the player is your son (especially in a high-level, highly competitive Division I program), a great deal of demands will be placed upon him. For example, he will have to be mature enough to accept the responsibility of performing well and work through the doubts and fears that might arise concerning keeping his spot on the team. He will have to be mentally tough, disciplined, and ready to be an adult...and act like one. No excuses will be acceptable—particularly not for being late, forgetful, or lazy. If he is weak in any of these areas, he will either grow up quickly, give in and quit, or the worst scenario of all, he will be asked to leave the team.

Tom Hanks, playing the role of a coach in *A League of Their Own* (a baseball movie about women-only leagues that were created during World War II) said to one of his players in the film, "Oh, you're crying. You can't cry. There is no crying in baseball!" Accordingly, as a diamond mom, when your son goes off to college, it's time for you to toughen up and be prepared for the rigors of a man's world in its most basic form, because college baseball is *truly* when the rubber meets the pavement for your son on his baseball journey. It is as close to military boot camp as it can be without having to send your son to war. As usual, you need to tuck your hankie away and toughen up. If your son is heading for college, you must be prepared not to cry.

The Reality and Upside of College

Once the recruiting process is complete, you will find that your son's entrance into a college as an athlete is a little more streamlined than it is for other students. Regardless of whether he is going to play in a four-year program or a community college, his registration for classes will typically be easier than it is for the general student population. More often than not, for example, most athletes are given scheduling preference so their class schedules fit into their baseball schedule.

The following information about the level of daily time commitments for collegiate baseball players, including attending classes, doing homework, studying for tests, and having time to eat meals, not to mention sleeping, is the equivalent to having two full-time jobs. You should be aware that the pressure your son feels is substantial, genuine, and at times, overwhelming.

As a collegiate player, your son will be required to expend no less than three hours (usually more) a day to baseball during the off-season and as many as six hours a day during the season. Many colleges play "fall ball." As a rule, fall-ball teams (prior to cuts) either play intrasquad games or other local area teams. Such competition offers a number of potential benefits, including giving the players a chance to adapt to their new environment, providing an opportunity for team members to bond, and allowing coaches to once again evaluate the playing ability of their players. Fall-ball teams are usually run by returning team leaders (because college baseball coaches are limited in the number of hours that they can spend with their players in the off-season). If such a program exists at the college your son attends, the number of hours of his commitment to baseball will increase. Another factor that can extend your son's time commitment to baseball is the fact that all players are encouraged and expected to participate in the team's conditioning program during the fall, so that they will be prepared physically once the spring season begins.

Although it can vary from school to school and situation to situation, for the most part, collegiate baseball is serious business. Your son should understand the fact that it is a privilege and an honor to play collegiate baseball. Furthermore, he should accept the fact that almost every coach wants players on his team who are dedicated and ready to wholeheartedly commit themselves to do their best, both academically *and* athletically. As a rule, your son will be given enough leeway to make or break his relationship with either his head coach or his school. On the other hand, he will also be put under a microscope in a way he has probably never experienced before.

Most players entering college are accustomed to being the top player in their communities. Given the fact that there are 2.4 million high school baseball players, and approximately 70,000 to 80,000 of those players enter college as players, it can easily be seen how college squads can be viewed as the "all-star" teams of high school players. While your son may have been a "natural" standout player in high school, once he enters college, the talent pyramid will begin all over again. Some players may be better than your son, while others may be less talented.

At this point in your son's baseball journey, he will be an all-star in a group with other all-stars, each one hungry for a starting position on the team. In reality, some players are more talented than others, some hungrier, some more dedicated, some better prepared for the challenges inherent in playing collegiate baseball, and some not quite so ready for them. To place it in a clearer perspective, imagine going to work for a company that only hired the top 25 sales representatives in your city or state.

Baseball also provides your son with a community he can be a part of when he begins college. He instantly has a group of friends who understand the pressures and demands he is facing in this situation. Once the team is established, an amazing level of camaraderie evolves among these young men. They truly become a family, with all the positives and negatives that being in a family involves. They support and empathize with each other; they fight and complain; and yet, they are always watching each other's back. They celebrate their successes and suffer their losses together. When the situation warrants it, they rally around a player who might be struggling—on or off the field. It is an amazing process to observe, a scenario that further reinforces the fact that baseball is indeed a "team" sport.

Arriving at School

If your son has made his college team and is not a walk-on or planning on trying out for the squad as a non-recruited player, he may be required to report to school earlier than his friends who are not student-athletes. For example, if he has been recruited by a top Division I school, he will be expected to show up on campus in August or September in shape and ready to play ball, even though the regular season is five months away.

One father once told me that because his son would be competing with older players at college, he suggested to him that he needed to be his best so the coach would play him. This concept may be motivational for some young men, but it is not honest. In reality, coaches do not expect 18-year-olds to be as developed or as mature as the 21-year-olds on their team. Quite frankly, some players are, and some are not. What coaches expect is that the confidence they have placed in your son be reciprocated by him with a resolute commitment to always give and do his best.

One way your son can demonstrate his commitment to excellence is to show up at the start of school in shape, ready to do whatever is asked of him. Failing to do so is a sure-fire recipe for hurting his chances of playing time. As a baseball mom, you need to let your son know if (in your opinion) he is acting in an irresponsible way (e.g., taking it easy, rather than working out). As such, you have several options for communicating your opinions to your son. Telling him the truth, regardless of his reaction, is certainly one way. *Demanding* that he exhibit a certain level of self-discipline and self-sacrifice the summer before he enters college is tempting, but rarely effective. Trying to establish a balanced, yet disciplined, work ethic in your son as he grows up may help the situation. On the other hand, you cannot redesign your son's personality any more than you can change the shape of an apple. At this point in time, your only obligation is to give him the information that can help him make informed choices. Beyond that, it is his responsibility to make sure that he is ready to play collegiate baseball, however that translates in his mind. As his mother, you should do what you can to help him to understand this concept and then let go.

Redshirts

By rule, each player has four years of eligibility as a college player. In other words, your son can play collegiate baseball for four seasons. Players do not necessarily use their four years of eligibility in consecutive years. For example, a player attending a Division I school who is injured in the first half of his season (or a Division II player injured at any time who has only played 20 percent of the year) can be given a medical hardship waiver (sometimes called a medical redshirt) and come back and play another season. The hardship year does not count against the four-year allowance.

The term "redshirt" is used when a player who is on the official roster of a collegiate team is not played in a live-game situation during the official season. In other words, he has not entered the game, as a starter or as a substitute, for even one play. If he is on the field for even 30 seconds, the NCAA will normally consider that he has expended one year of his playing eligibility. Players have five years (and in rare and unique situations, six years) in which to use their four years of eligibility. Redshirting is a procedure that is designed to allow coaches the opportunity to mold the players to their programs, helping to build and maintain strong player rosters for the future.

Sometimes, an incoming freshman player is disappointed when a coach redshirts him, especially when the player's hopes are high, and he is looking forward to continuing to play baseball, following the summer of his high school graduation. Most high school graduates, especially when entering a Division I collegiate program, are not quite yet mature enough either emotionally or physically to compete against their 21-year-old teammates. As a result, many talented players are occasionally redshirted during their freshman year. Being redshirted is not a disgraceful situation, only a disappointing one. While being redshirted may not be easy for your son, his coach may actually be doing him a favor. Redshirts can practice with the team and participate in intrasquad scrimmages, and still be a huge part of the baseball community.

The decision to redshirt a player is made by the head coach. However, if after a relatively substantial period of time a player recognizes he will get no time on the field of play during a season, he can go directly to the coach and request to be redshirted. Hopefully, his coach would respond by complying with that player's request; most would, in my opinion. A player who is in this situation where he is unsure about whether he should ask the coach to redshirt him should discuss the circumstances with someone who can provide him with much-needed insight, perspective, and advice before he takes any action. At the very least, the player should probably wait until the season is at least half over before making such a request to his coach. It is important to note that if a player is redshirted (either for reasons related to lack of playing or for medical reasons), he is still considered part of the team and, as such, falls under the rules and regulations of the appropriate governing body (NCAA or NAIA and of the school).

Grayshirting

The term "grayshirting" is a slang term being used by some community colleges. While this term is not widely used, it should raise a "red flag" (not to be mistaken for "redshirt") for you. If some school or coach attempts to place such a tag on your son, you should seek clarification of your son's playing eligibility from someone in a position of authority (his coach or the athletic director of his school), preferably in writing.

Choosing a College

■ *Community College.* There are literally thousands of community colleges (also known as junior colleges) sprinkled across America. It could easily be argued that many students would end with their educational journey at the high school level, were it not for these institutions. Community colleges provide a place for students to complete their core courses (e.g., English, math, science) before they transfer to a four-year college of their choice. Junior colleges also provide technical training for those students who have little interest in obtaining a four-year degree. All factors considered, junior colleges are a hotbed for baseball players.

There are a number of reasons why high school baseball players who are graduating might consider attending junior colleges as student-athletes. For some students, the transition from high school to junior college and then to a four-year college is a less demanding and more logical education progression. For these students, the ability to make any needed academic adjustments is much easier. While this sequence may be a logical evolutionary pathway for some student-athletes, many baseball players attend junior colleges for one reason and one reason alone. They can be drafted into the major leagues in either their freshman or sophomore year at a junior college, whereas if they are attending a four-year institution, they are not eligible for the major league draft until the summer following their junior year.

One of the biggest mistakes junior college baseball players make is that they often downplay the importance of achieving good grades. They should remember that they are still students first, and grades will be as important as they ever have been if they are to continue to play baseball past their completion of junior college. While a player may be thinking he will be drafted by the major leagues from junior college, in all likelihood, he will not. Accordingly, if he wants to play baseball past his junior- college experience (NCAA regulations deem a player can only play baseball at the community college level for two years), he will need to have decent grades if he plans to transfer to a four-year college.

The requirements for community college players to transfer into a four-year college are somewhat complex and depend on so many variables that it is too difficult to list them in this book. As such, those junior college student-athletes who want to continue playing at a four-year university should contact the NCAA and order a transfer guide that is updated each year. In any number of ways, this book can serve as an invaluable guide for junior college athletes and can be quite helpful in ensuring that the transfer process is successful.

One last piece of advice would be to have your son to be in constant communication with his coach and his junior college counselor regarding the courses he should take in school and the transferability of any credits he earns to four-year schools. Not taking appropriate course work could sideline him from playing for a year, while he gets his academic requirements up to speed. *One final piece of advice that bears repeating is that you should remind your son that he is a student playing baseball, not a baseball player who happens to be a student.*

■ *Four-Year Colleges.* Four-year colleges that are NCAA members are grouped into three basic levels: Division I, Division II, and Division III, each with its own rules and regulations. Irrespective of what category of school at which students attend, they must maintain a 2.0 grade point average in college (as in high school) to be eligible to play during the season. If the coaches are going to invest time, energy, manpower, training, and any other numerous amounts of resources on your son, they want to be sure that he will take his education seriously. In reality, life exists after baseball, and your son will need to be prepared for it. In fact, most college coaches are aware of and appreciate this fact better than almost anyone else.

As a rule, Division I colleges tend to attract the majority of the top student-athletes, individuals whose grade-point average out of high school is at least 3.0+ and whose baseball ability is above average. If your son has a lower GPA than the published admission standards for a particular school a possibility exists that he still might be admitted to that school, depending on how and if that institution wants your son to play baseball for it. If it does, however, your son will be on academic probation during his first year of attendance at that school. Division I schools actively and aggressively recruit players from both high school and community colleges. While Division II and III schools approach their baseball programs seriously, as you can imagine, the talent pool is typically somewhat less deep at both the Division II (compared with Division I) and the Division III level (as compared with Division II).

If a player decides that he wants to leave any NCAA college baseball program and transfer to another NCAA program, he will find that the rules governing such a transfer vary between Division I and Division II and III schools. *The transfer rules pertaining to this situation are clear-cut and uncompromising.* It can't be emphasized too much, however, that if your son is faced with such a decision, it is essential that he takes the time to thoroughly familiarize himself with the NCAA rules on transfers. Under no circumstances should you allow him to take a particular action because "someone told (him) what to do." He should obtain the NCAA rulebook and if he doesn't understand it, he should contact the NCAA and get the necessary assistance. A transfer that is done either improperly or illegally (based on a disregard for NCAA rules) can get your son disqualified from playing and may harm the school to which he transfers. A claim of ignorance after the fact is no excuse.

Moms and College

Whether the situation involves your first child going off to college or your last, it is never easy letting your child rush off to a new adventure on his own. On the other hand, there are some potential blessings if your son lives away from you, because, all factors considered, you undoubtedly will be less stressed not being fully aware of the day-in, day-out activities of your son's new life.

In general, parenting adult children seems to be far more challenging than parenting young children. The difference is quite clear, actually. With small children, we are so exhausted that we literally "die" into bed at night and sleep soundly once they are tucked in. With grown children, we stay up all night worrying about them. Either way, we wind up exhausted.

Communication is essential to the success of any relationship, particularly one between you and your son. Open, honest communication during this phase of his baseball journey is an absolute necessity. He must understand what is expected of him with regard to such important matters as his grades, behavior, accountability, finances, etc. At times, you may need to devote more than the usual amount of patience with him, as he is transported on a seemingly never-ending roller coaster ride. On the other hand, if he is fortunate enough to play baseball in college, you will be in for the time of your life.

12

It's Not Over Until the Fat Lady Sings

"It ain't over till it's over."

— Yogi Berra

Baseball is an eternal fountain of hope. Usually, a team does not consider itself defeated until the last out of the last inning of the game...even if it has been held scoreless to that point. In baseball, the tide of good fortune can turn towards the losing team at any point. The fickle finger of fate sometimes affects other aspects of baseball as well. For example, on occasion, a good player might go unnoticed in college and may feel the opportunity to play professional ball is closed to them. On the other hand, if they have the seeds of determination and the willingness to knock on doors until someone answers, they may make their way to the "bigs"...assuming their skills are above average, they possess a high level of fitness, and they exhibit a resolute passion for the game.

With regard to playing baseball professionally, if your son does not sign a professional baseball contract and has completed college, he will have a few options, including signing as an undrafted free agent, signing a contract with an independent team, and participating in one or more of the various tryouts that take place around the country, hoping scouts will take notice and offer him the opportunity to play.

The first option, to sign as an undrafted free agent, is easier if local-area scouts are familiar with your son. Like most professions, personal relationships often are the key to anyone's success. Baseball is not an exception to that reality. As a rule, most professional major league organizations will usually sign a couple of players after the professional spring draft has been completed in order to "fill out their rosters." Basically, what that means is that there are often spots on minor-league team rosters where players are needed.

The second option, signing with an independent-league team, will also provide your son with the opportunity to continue to play baseball. There are numerous independent leagues in every area of the United States. Among the most well-known independent leagues are the following (by region): (Midwest) Northern and Frontier Leagues, (New York) Atlantic League, (Louisiana/Texas) Central League, and (California) Golden Baseball League. You can search the Internet for lists of the independent leagues by entering the words *"independent baseball leagues"* in your web browser. Independent league teams are not affiliated with Major League Baseball. On the other hand, some players have been drafted from these leagues into professional baseball over the years.

The third option—which involves attending major league camps (usually during the month of February) with the hope of being signed as a minor-league free agent—is, frankly, a long shot. What it is, no doubt, is vivid testimony to the willingness and dedication of players willing to chase their dream to its end. The movie, *"The Rookie"* staring Dennis Quaid, is an example of this process at work. The movie depicts the true-life story of Jimmy Morris, a high school teacher, baseball coach, and former professional player, who makes a promise to his high school players that if they win their District championship, he will try out for baseball again. Ultimately, he finds himself in a position of having to do as he promised. He then locates a "major league camp," whereupon he shows up with his three children for a tryout. The movie's

Hollywood ending depicts him being recruited to play for the Tampa Bay Devil Rays. Morris eventually played for the Tampa Bay Devil Rays, and his story is inspirational because it involved a good man, whose hard work beat the odds. As has been stated several times previously in this book, dreams can and do occasionally come true (particularly in the movies). The more pertinent part of the movie is the depiction of what he had to sacrifice, given his circumstances, to have the opportunity.

If your son has completed college and still has a desire to play professional baseball, he can pursue his dreams on his own. The real challenge is that any player coming out of college unrecruited must work harder and be more dedicated than anyone else. In the above-mentioned story, Jimmy Morris was a left-handed pitcher who had a 98-mph fastball. In reality, the ability to throw a pitch as hard as Jimmy Morris is not necessarily the baseline measuring stick for your son to evaluate himself against. On the other hand, if your son has talent, (and given the right set of circumstances) scouts may eventually notice.

If your son chooses to pursue his dream of having a professional baseball career after college, his most immediate issue will be finances. Obviously, he will be blessed if you, as his parent, are willing to help finance his dream. If he has to do it on his own, the strength of his resolve will be tested. Unquestionably, his pathway will be far more difficult.

The most important factor in making a decision whether your son should pursue a professional career after college is his level of talent. Is your son a big enough fish to swim in the talent pool of players who will be trying out for professional teams? If he can answer "yes" to this question, then the next issue that needs to be addressed is: does he have what it takes in self-discipline, perseverance, focus, and patience to make the most of his circumstances and opportunities?

Going Forward

If your son is serious about pursuing alternative paths into the world of professional baseball, he should try to make whatever connection he can with scouts and other professionals in the industry. If that option is unavailable, he can visit the Major League Baseball website (www.mlb.com). If your son is looking for dates and times for tryouts, this information can be located by entering the word "tryouts" in the search key found at the bottom of the home page. Your son can also sign up for Pro Baseball Tryouts (a membership site that is available online at www.probaseballtryouts.com for a small annual fee) and receive information on the various tryouts around the United States.

How You Can Help

Most young men fresh out of college will have to have another job while they wait for the opportunity to try out for a professional baseball team. *If your son requests your assistance*, you can help him by doing some research and seeking out times, dates, and places for tryouts. As mentioned earlier in this chapter, you may also choose to offer financial assistance to your son. If you are willing and able to do this, your son should consider himself very fortunate.

The good-news aspect of your son's attempts to continue playing baseball is that one day he may actually become a professional baseball player. The bad-news feature of the scenario is that the minor leagues do not pay well. In addition, his progression through the ranks of minor league baseball may be drawn out and time-consuming. There seem to be as many levels in the minor league system as there are in bureaucratic government. The system begins with the minor or rookie league and ascends to low A ball, high A ball, AA ball, AAA ball, and then the majors. While making it through the ranks and becoming a major league baseball player may ultimately result in a player being awarded with a sizable financial stipend, the truth is that getting there can be quite painful, with many players forced to live at a near poverty income. Having a supplemental job while playing is almost impossible due to the level of commitment a player must make during the season. As a result, many players must sustain themselves on as little as $800 a month.

If your son decides he still wants to pursue his dream of baseball, then you will need to address potentially the hardest issue of all: are you willing to help support your son financially? If the answer to that question is "yes," then more pointed and equally serious questions need to be asked. How long will you be willing to support his dream and at what cost to you? How long is he asking for support? How much can you afford to give, and will it be a loan or a gift? There are circumstances when a player could end up in the minor league system for as long as eight years. Accordingly, it is essential that you consider the possibilities and probabilities as you enter into a "business partnership" with your son. The length of time you decide to help fund your son's extended baseball journey and the degree of financial commitment you choose to make will have to be carefully considered and planned.

The Last Out

A time may eventually occur when you may have to call the last strike in the last inning to end the game. In other words, facing the end of your son's baseball journey may be difficult, not only for your son, but also for you. It may be hard on your whole family. I only considered adding this section after interviewing a mother who faced this situation and who had to decide, together with her husband, whether to continue supporting her son. They chose to support their son. Not every family has the luxury, willingness, or ability to make such a decision. The best advice I can offer you if confronted by similar circumstances is to first be honest about your son's ability and then, finally, listen to your heart. Or better yet, listen to your stomach. Deepak Chopra contends that listening to your gut is far more advisable than listening to your thoughts, since your gut has not learned to argue with you yet.

13

Why Pitch Count Counts

You win some;
You lose some;
You wreck some.

— David Baird
A Thousand Paths to Wisdom

Regardless of their position, I love to watch players in a game. Seeing a double-play turned, an outstanding catch by an outfielder, a steal of home, or double-drives in runs represent one of the purest forms of entertainment available to mankind. Pitchers, however hold a special place in my heart. I am, after all, the mother of a pitcher. While every position deserves to be recognized, catchers and pitchers seem to have the most physically challenging positions on the team. (Being a pitcher's mother tends to make my focus more pointed.) In the 15 years that I have observed pitchers, I have had the opportunity to witness the good, the bad, and the ugly.

Because a pitcher's arm is involved in *every single play of the game*, the subject of how a coach uses a pitcher in a game is an issue about which I have heartfelt opinions. In the extreme, I am personally aware of a 14-year-old with a future in baseball that was destroyed by an overzealous coach who once had him throw 160 pitches in the game. At the time, I empathized with the parents. Their son was in a very competitive baseball program, and they felt trapped between their need to protect their son and their desire to honor his efforts to be part of a very demanding varsity squad. Unfortunately, his arm was "blown out" long before he even got a chance to play for varsity. His story is not unusual. Far too often, the need to win can cause strain and dissent between parents, their sons, and their coaches. Hopefully, the reason that the aforementioned story is so abhorrent will be apparent to you by the end of this chapter.

Dr. Tom House has made it one of his life pursuits to seek documented evidence that will help convince coaches and parents, alike, that an overly abused arm can lead to the demise of a pitcher. From Little League to college, regardless of your son's age, an overused arm can kill his chances of ever being considered by coaches, college recruiters, or scouts. Accordingly, as your son's mother and advocate, you *must* make sure that the people in his life who matter most to him are aware of this fact. Mostly, you *must* educate your son about what constitutes placing too much stress on his body, so he can properly take care of himself.

Being sensitive to the potential "fragility" of the human body is very important. Unfortunately, it is a factor that many athletes are either unaware of or simply choose to ignore, including baseball players. All baseball players, especially pitchers, have the hero's archetype. In *Joseph Campbell: The Power of Myth* with Bill Moyers, Campbell talks about the archetype of the "hero" being present in most people. To a degree, everyone is on a hero's journey, but none more than a baseball player defending his team's right to win. Every one of our sons who plays baseball wants to be the one to hit the ball out of the park for the winning home run; every one of our sons who pitches wants to be the one who strikes out the last batter, with the bases loaded, in the bottom of the ninth inning to win a one-run ballgame (regardless of pitch count). Figuratively, our sons perceive themselves as the Luke Skywalkers or Hans Solos of the diamond. Such a vision, however, can blind them to the reality they are human and need to take care of their bodies.

A Walk in Moccasins

The following experiment can help illustrate the fact that repetitive demands on the body can be quite fatiguing. *(Note: You should perform this experiment only if you are healthy and have no physical limitations or concerns.)* The experiment requires you to open and close your fingers; make a fist, then extend your fingers out fully and then close them again into a fist. Do this 100 times. If you are able to complete the required number of repetitions, you will feel the muscles in your hands and forearms tiring. If you are unable to do this exercise as requested, try to remember what carrying a seven-pound baby around in your arms for even 20 minutes felt like. Remember how your arms tired and how, when you put the baby down, your arms and shoulders ached? It didn't matter how fit were, you experienced tired muscles, much like you will if you perform the experiment.

Doing anything repetitively for too long can cause pain. Your muscles may become sore, and your joints may ache. Muscle fatigue, when you are a pitcher, can be very serious stuff. Unfortunately, all too often, such fatigue is ignored or dismissed by coaches who are more interested in their team getting an out or a win than they are in the arms of the young men in their care. Any coach who places undue stress on your son's arm is a fraud. He either doesn't know better, or he is masquerading as someone who has the team's and your son's best interests at heart. Most certainly, he is not the coach your son needs or deserves. Too often, coaches with this kind of mentality try to mask these misguided actions with morally bankrupt claims that they are "trying to make a man out of your son." Bull-hooey! More likely, what they are doing is taking your son's future out of the game he loves.

The bottom line is that if your son is a pitcher and his coach is abusing him, you must do what is necessary to stop the abuse as quickly as possible. While high school is the primary opportunity for colleges to observe your son, he will have the opportunity to be seen in other venues if you research his options and act accordingly. For example, summer teams, scout teams, and showcases (all levels) offer your son opportunities to be seen. Regardless of the feedback/pressure/displeasure you might receive from your son, you must do whatever you can to protect him from a coach who places excessive demands on his arm.

Both medical science and experience show that the joints and tendons of the body are not indestructible anatomical structures, capable of withstanding repetitive, unduly stressful work. For example, consider all of the people who experience carpal tunnel syndrome from keyboarding all day long. Furthermore, typing on a computer keyboard is not, by design, a violent, aggressive act. It is simply repetitive. On the other hand, imagine the same repetitive action, only with significant load forces, on an arm. Take it a step further and envision the arm attached to a growing body, a body whose growth plates are not even closed, a body that is still "under construction." The key point that should be derived from this situation is simply that "too much of anything is not a good thing."

What You See Is Not All There Is

Pitching a baseball can be somewhat of an illusion. We observe the pitcher's arm throwing the ball. As such, a pitcher stands on the mound and throws the ball toward home plate. We see his arm come up to his face, drop in a motion toward home plate, and subsequently release the ball.

The lyrics from the old song, *"The hipbone's connected to the thigh bone, the thigh bone's connected to the knee bone, the knee bone's connected to…"* provides a more apt message of the actual scenario that is occurring. In reality, if a pitcher tries to depend solely upon his arm to get the ball over the plate, he is writing himself a one-way ticket out of baseball.

Regrettably, if your son is strong and can throw hard he may over-depend on his arm and dismiss the value of proper training. You must not let such a scenario happen. If you are the mother of a pitcher, there are two areas you should be particularly conscious of in this regard:

- the importance of an overall conditioning and training program
- the importance of sound pitching mechanics

A sound, conditioning program for a pitcher involves more than simply taking care of his arm (and shoulder and elbow). His workout regimen must also include exercises for the muscles of his back, abdomen, buttocks, and legs, as well as activities that will enhance his levels of both his cardiovascular (heart-lung) fitness and flexibility. In other words, a properly designed program focuses on total fitness, not just an isolated fitness component. In reality, it takes the whole body to keep the pitcher healthy. Tom House is a strong proponent of the fact that a player is only as strong as his weakest link (think of the body as a chain). For example, if a right-handed pitcher's left side is underdeveloped it will be unable to support the stress placed on the right side of his body—balance, balance, balance.

The mental side of the baseball also has a critical impact on how well a pitcher performs. In the immortal words of the ever-so eloquent Yogi Berra, "Baseball is 90 percent mental. The other half is physical." The implications and applications of the mental aspects of the game are virtually endless. For example, a pitcher has to have short-term memory loss when he's pitching because if he doesn't, he sinks himself by thinking about what he just did (e.g., gave up a home run), rather than focusing on what he must do (e.g., get the next batter out).

Dominick Johnson, my son's high school pitching coach, once said to me, "If you don't believe in yourself, you're not going to give yourself the best chance to succeed." He followed up by stating, "The mental part of baseball is the most important part of the game. The mental aspects of baseball involve more than just being mentally strong. It is also important that pitchers understand their position, how to play it, are able to recognize common strategic situations that might arise (such as a hitter preparing to bunt the ball), and to know what to do if and when they do." In reality, pitchers often have to make split-second decisions when they are on the mound. If they are worrying about being perfect for any reason or anyone, they can place insurmountable obstacles in their way.

A Pitcher's Objective

A pitcher's job is to get the ball over the plate, throwing to an area about the size of a file storage box. (Note: A hitter's strike zone is the width of home plate and the height between a player's chest and his knees. In reality, on occasion, a few umpires liberally define this zone. As a result, some pitchers report being exhausted at the end of a game because the umpire's strike zone was ill-defined.) Anyway…back to the pitcher. The pitcher must throw a five-ounce ball 60 feet, six inches (closer for youth baseball) as hard as he can, as accurately as he can. Should your son pitch multiple innings, he may have to do this as many as 60-to-100 times over the course of an entire game. Ideally, each time he throws the ball he will use the same muscles, the same tendons, the same mechanics…over, and over, and over, and over again. In fact, even a highly conditioned athlete can only withstand the load forces to which he is subjecting his body for so long. The key issue that arises in this regard is how long is too long?

How Many Is Too Many?

Every pitcher has a relative ceiling concerning the number of pitches he can throw before he subjects his body to an excessive level of stress. That number can vary somewhat, depending on the pitcher and his level of conditioning. For the most part, however, the magic number is approximately 100. You can begin to count seriously if your son has pitched eight innings and his pitch count is reaching 100. As a measuring stick, the number 100 applies to college pitchers; it is somewhat lower for both high school and adolescent pitchers.

For some pitchers, the ceiling for the recommended number of pitches will be less; for others, it will be more. The key point is that you must determine what the appropriate number of pitches for your son to throw is. Table 13.1, based on information provided by Tom House and the National Pitching Association (NPA), can serve as a guideline for you.

It is important that your son is educated about not overusing his arm when he is young. Such education is not a back-channel way of advocating that you or your son "baby" his arm. Rather, it is a well-grounded suggestion that you share knowledge with him, based on science, which will help extend his career and allow him to rise to his highest level of achievement, whether he is playing in high school, college, or professional baseball.

PITCH COUNT GUIDELINES

- 15-20: The average number of pitches per inning
- 60-75: The average number of pitches a peewee should have per game
- 75-90: The average number of pitches a high school player should have per game
- 90-115: The average number of pitches a collegiate or professional player should have per game

Table 13.1. Recommended pitch-count guidelines

On occasion, a pitcher might have a tough outing and end up throwing 25 pitches in a particular inning. On the other hand, if he winds up throwing fewer pitches in his following inning, his total number of pitches will eventually balance out. Responsible coaches not only count pitches, they also watch to see where in the game a pitcher's pitch count is up. If he is struggling early, he may just be settling down and need an inning or so to adjust. By the same token, if his pitcher is struggling later in the game (e.g., his pitch count is high in the seventh inning), then the coach might discern that his pitcher is tired. If you are keeping track of the pitch count, you might also determine that your son may be tiring. Such knowledge and appreciation of the game, on your part, might help your son be more likely to understand the situation should his coach choose to pull him from a well-pitched game.

Your son's coach will not be your only potential obstacle when ensuring you're your son (the pitcher) does not overuse his arm. You will also be confronted with another challenge—your son. Regardless of his pitch count, if he is doing well, he will typically not want to leave the game. As such, it is important to help your son understand the concept of "tomorrow" and why it has meaning in his life. A responsible coach, if he is worth his salt, will assist you in this regard by always disregarding the pitcher's pleadings to remain in the game (on the mound) when the coach knows that his pitcher has gone as far as he should.

Once a pitcher has thrown as many pitches as his body can reasonably and safely endure, his muscles go into a condition that is referred to as "muscle failure." Once a pitcher experiences muscle failure, his muscles weaken and become vulnerable. In reference to the previously cited example of the situation when you were carrying your seven-pound bundle of joy around in your arms for any extended period of time, seven pounds is not particularly heavy. On the other hand, if you carry seven pounds in your arms for an extended period of time, your muscles will become fatigued. Even though your son is only throwing a five-ounce sphere through the air, his actions exert incredible force on his elbow and shoulder. Eventually, his muscles, much like yours when you carried him for too long as a tiny infant, give out.

According to Dr. Tom House, once your son, as a pitcher, gets into muscle failure, every pitch he throws after that is equivalent to three pitches. In other words, for every pitch he throws, his muscles react as if he has thrown three. If your son begins to experience muscle failure at 75 pitches and he goes in for two more innings (throwing 15 pitches per inning), his muscles will react as if he has thrown 90 extra pitches (using the 3-x rule) after pitching just two more innings. While he technically has thrown 105 pitches, his body will respond as if he has thrown 165 pitches. On the other hand, he is young, right? He can bounce back…If only it were that easy.

While a pitcher who throws an excessive number of pitches may not feel overly stressed on the day that he extends himself, his arm will have a hard time recovering from such a game without a fair amount of rest. Most "starters" (a term used to define the pitchers who are designated to start a game and complete as many innings as possible) tend to pitch at least once a week, some once every four days. A pitcher who is overly extended is literally pushed into a state of "physical deficit" that can compromise his ability to recover before his next outing. As a rule, he will likely go into his next pitch outing in a deficient state that will only grow from game to game.

When the coaching staff at the National Pitching Association works with pitchers and their parents, they provide moms (and dads) with pitch counters and ask them to monitor the pitch counts of their sons. The NPA's efforts are designed to help make parents acutely aware of the need for pitchers (at any age) not to exceed a reasonable/appropriate pitch count.

Serving as your son's advocate with regard to not allowing his arm to be overused is critical. At the present time, coaches seem to be becoming more and more aware of the need to protect a pitcher's arm. For those coaches who either ignore documented evidence or simply are too thickheaded to see the obvious, it is the parent's responsibility to help increase their awareness. The only way to do that is for parents to pay attention and, when a pitcher is being abused, become a very loud, very squeaky wheel. Just remember to squeak in a dignified, respectful manner!

Your Son's Job

Again, and it cannot be said too emphatically, it is not my intention to suggest that you over-protect your son or baby him in any way. In reality, if your son is to be a pitcher, he has to work out twice as hard as anyone else (other than the catcher) on the team. It is his responsibility to be prepared. The challenge with many young, talented individuals is that these players are typically above-average athletes when they are throwing in high school. On the other hand, if and when they make a college team, they will be among the crème-de-la crème. The demands upon their bodies will be increased, not only physically, but mentally and emotionally as well. A pampered athlete will find it very difficult (if not impossible) to survive the rigors of college or professional ball. Not surprisingly, college coaches want players who are prepared and ready to work—on and off the baseball field.

To play in high school, college, and beyond, a player must do what is necessary to keep himself "in the game." In that regard, the best (and the safest *and* smartest, in my opinion) workout materials for pitchers can be found at the National Pitching Association's website—www.nationalpitching.com. Featuring programs designed by sport scientists and professionals who focus on providing players with sound advice, the NPA offers balanced, proven approaches for in-season and off-season training.

A Losing Proposition

It is important that you are aware of the fact that it is normal and expected that your son will lose baseball games. It is wonderful when pitchers have winning seasons, and good ones usually do. On the other hand, even winning pitchers occasionally lose a game or two...or more. Such are the nuances of the sport where a pitcher can have a wonderful game, even throw several shutout innings, and still lose by a close contest.

As a mother, the best thing you can do concerning your son's on-the-field performance is to celebrate his wins and outstanding performances and empathize quietly with him over his losses and disappointments. One of my favorite sayings that applies to this situation is, "A silent mouth is sweet to hear." In discussing this issue with one of my friends, her experience in this area was very reassuring to me. By giving her son space to process his own feelings about his performance, she found that he eventually did come to her and her husband. Neither of them initiated conversations with him after a tough game, but they were always available when he wanted to talk or needed a shoulder on which to lean. On one hand, staying silent or waiting when you know your son needs comforting can be challenging, but on the other hand, it is important to establish an environment where your son knows he can reach out to you when and if he wants to. More often than not, your son does not want to be comforted; he simply wants to comprehend his circumstances and the situation surrounding them.

There is an analogy involving a caterpillar that can help teach a powerful parenting skill. One day, a person noticed a cocoon breaking open and a butterfly emerging, struggling to free itself. Feeling sorry for the butterfly's struggle, the person assisted the butterfly and helped free it. The person's assistance only served to weaken the butterfly. Its wings were underdeveloped, and it was too weak to fly. Instead of experiencing its life as a butterfly, it died in the person's hand. While the individual's intentions were good and well-intended, those "good" intentions ended up being fatal for the butterfly.

In a similar vein, if your son has learned to trust that you will listen to him, and if you can wait until he feels he is ready and can trust that he has the inner strength to confront and deal with his challenges, then eventually he will come to you. By not trying to free him from his proverbial cocoon and by letting him struggle a bit with the challenges of life (on and off the baseball diamond), his "wings" will be stronger, thereby ensuring his ability to fly. Besides, it's best to save your voice for things that really matter, like setting curfews and establishing boundaries of behavior.

14

Coping With Injuries

"It isn't the mountains ahead to climb that wear you out;
it's the pebble in your shoe."

— Muhammad Ali

I was watching a baseball game against our cross-town rival when my son was a sophomore in high school. It was a bright sunny spring day that was achingly close to summer. The pitcher for the opposing team was a very gifted left-hander who had kept our offensive players at bay for a number of innings. Our team was playing tough, and we were at bat.

The pitcher went into his windup and while his arm was midway through his delivery, it simply dropped to his side. The pitch he had just thrown flew to the top of the backstop, and the crowd looked in bewilderment as the pitcher just stood there. Soon, players and coaches were hustling to his side, and he left the game. It took doctors three days to figure out what was wrong. He had a cyst that had burst on a bone in his arm, and he was out of baseball until his senior year.

It was frightening to see his arm drop. I identified and sympathized with the player and his parents. The young athlete was preparing to enter his junior year of high school, the year when colleges begin looking for future players. Fortunately, because of exceptionally skilled doctors and a healthy, wise, and well-scripted recuperating program, this situation had a happy ending. He was drafted by a professional team right out of high school and is currently doing well in his major league organization.

His experience was relevant to me for at least two reasons. First, until that moment, the only similar situation that my husband and I had experienced involved a mild case of tendonitis in our son's elbow. At that point, I learned that serious injuries could be part of baseball. Second, while the player's injury was fairly severe, with proper medical treatment and a responsible, recuperative program, he was able to come back. I learned that even extreme situations could be rectified, given the right set of circumstances.

Injuries are a reality in any sport. Accordingly, you have to expect that your son will experience some kind of injury if he plays baseball. If you like to rely on statistics, basically, your son's odds of being hurt are more than a golfer, but less than a football player. According to Personal Health Zone (a website dedicated to news and information on health, fitness, and alternative medicine), more than 500,000 baseball-related injuries are treated in hospitals, clinics, and emergency rooms each year. While that figure might seem startling, it represents less than 10 percent of those who play baseball each year. Furthermore, many of those injuries are undoubtedly not serious.

In reality, it is not the injuries that your son might suffer, but the decisions you make regarding the treatment of his injuries that can make the difference between whether he has a long or a shortened career. In this instance, everybody's grandmother's advice is quite applicable, "an ounce of prevention is worth a pound of cure."

It should be noted that the information presented in this chapter is not meant to be a replacement for medical treatment advice from your physician. In fact, any injury of consequence your son incurs should be regarded most seriously, and your physician and health practitioners should be consulted immediately. On the other hand, who knows your son better than you? Some people have higher pain thresholds than others. In turn, if your son has a relatively low (or non-existent) threshold of pain, you should assess each situation accordingly. As such, the body has three basic lines of defense: muscle first, connective tissue second, and bone last. Accordingly, if an injury is bone-related, you should realize that the other "defenses" of the body have broken down, and the injury is relatively serious. Because each injury is unique, it is important for your son to be knowledgeable about the kinds and degrees of injuries that can occur so he knows how to prevent them, but if they do happen, how to treat them in an effective manner. In reality, when injuries occur, they should be treated emotionally and mentally, as well as physically.

Common Baseball Injuries

The "itises" seem to raise their ugly heads more than any other injury when it comes to baseball. Tendons attach muscles to bones. They tend to be stiffer and denser than the muscles and lack elasticity. Constant pulling or stress can cause small tears at microscopic levels, resulting in inflammation, pain, and the condition known as tendonitis.

The "itis" can strike any player, but pitchers and catchers tend to be a little more prone to tendonitis than other players, simply because they are throwing a ball on every play of the game. The repeated use of a joint—the elbow and shoulder for a pitcher and the knees, elbow, and shoulder for a catcher—increases the possibility of injury. Any inflammatory condition can cut like a knife and be (to say the least) distracting to a player. If you have ever experienced "tennis elbow," you can relate to the discomfort that accompanies tendonitis. The most common areas of the body afflicted with tendonitis are the elbow, wrist, biceps, shoulder (including rotator cuff attachments), leg, knee, ankle, hip, and Achilles tendon.

Even mild cases of tendonitis can limit the effectiveness of a player. Mistreated or ignored, it can lead to more serious injury. Accordingly, you must seek professional guidance if your son suffers from a chronic case of tendonitis.

Another common ailment that baseball players experience is groin pulls, which are often caused by a lack of flexibility and sufficient stretching. Athletes can employ a number of techniques and exercise modalities to help them stretch, including yoga, which many baseball players incorporate as part of their basic conditioning training. Remember how your parents used to have to warm up the engine of their car before they put it into gear? The human body faces a similar situation, in that it needs to be warmed and stretched prior to being asked to perform. Other common injuries that occur in baseball include, but are not limited to, back strains, broken fingers, concussions, welts from being hit by balls, etc.

If your son is a minor (i.e., under the age of 18) and you are responsible for his health, you should establish a relationship with an orthopedic physician. Whenever we felt it was appropriate, we have augmented the medical services we have attempted to provide for our son, including the use of chiropractors and naturopaths. Some families have been known to turn to acupuncture for help. The key point is that if at all possible, you should try to have your son's injury treated without invasive surgery. In reality, however, surgery is occasionally the only answer. In the case of the player I referred to previously in this chapter, surgery was the only answer. Once his body was surgically repaired, he pursued physical therapy and other alternative and natural remedies and programs that helped him regain his strength and effectiveness on the mound.

Surgery for Injuries

Since injuries can sometimes be serious, surgery can never be eliminated as a necessary option. If a doctor has prescribed surgery for your son, it is certainly appropriate and recommended that you get at least one (and preferably two) other professional opinions. That way, if one physician recommends surgery and another one does not, you know that you need to look into the matter further. While conservative recuperation is always an option, sometimes it is not viable.

On occasion, the simple act of exploratory arthroscopic surgery may be helpful to your injured son, not only physically, but also mentally and emotionally. It is recommended that you discuss any course of action with your son to find out how he feels about his situation and what path seems most feasible to him, even if he is relatively young. A nutritional program that includes recovery-related, doctor-prescribed drugs and/or nutritional supplementation for the joints, such as glucosamine and chondroitin, should also be part of his recuperative regimen. Even more so than usual, he should also hydrate his body often.

Aerobic Exercise and Recovery

Aerobic exercise can facilitate the recovery process by providing blood, oxygen, and nutrients to the body's cells and tissue that need them. Whether your son is recovering between games or from a serious injury, he should be engaging (with the exception of a situation where he has an orthopedic condition that would preclude such participation) in an aerobic-exercise program that will place an increased level of demands on his cardiovascular and circulatory systems.

The Mental/Emotional Equation

In reality, a serious injury can end your son's baseball career. Certainly, the previously mentioned player must have had that possibility running through his mind at the time when he was injured. Regardless of how old your son is when an injury occurs, if he is ever faced with having to deal with a situation involving a career-ending injury, it is absolutely essential that you are there to support him.

The ability to deal with adversity is one of the strongest attributes that anyone can develop during their lifetime. While your son deals with adversity on the baseball field most every time he steps on it, dealing with dramatic change is atypical for him. While some people are naturally more resilient than others, it is important to help your son realize that there is always a tomorrow. In fact, knowing, understanding, and believing this point can make a significant difference between a thorough recovery for your son from his injury and a lingering injury from which he never fully recovers.

If you find that you have reached an emotional impasse (wall) when it comes to your son's recuperation, have lost hope in the process, or feel somewhat bewildered in your role as a support and counseling system for your son, you should seek help and guidance from a third party. It is essential that you do whatever you need to do to help buoy first yourself and then your son. Fortunately, a number of excellent resources exist (refer to the appendices in the back of this book and to the Internet) that can help you through tough times, emotionally and mentally. Because, as the words of Annie (in Thomas Meeham's heart-rending play) so aptly declared, "the sun *will* come up tomorrow." As such, you should be prepared to welcome and embrace each and every tomorrow.

15

It's Not About Diet, It's About Fuel

"Let food be your medicine and medicine be your food."

— Hippocrates

It makes sense that as women, we profoundly influence our children when it comes to food, and yet our culture doesn't seem to promote a clear understanding of the fundamental differences between food and nutrition. One thing is certain, however: the image we hold of ourselves and how we nurture our physical bodies create a pattern that our children will adapt to their own lives. The choices that we make in our lives are analogous to being pens full of indelible ink, writing messages on the minds and hearts of our sons and daughters—messages of likes vs. dislikes, variety vs. sameness, healthy vs. unhealthy, etc.

As the mother, you are still probably the primary individual who is planning meals in your home, preparing snacks, and making sure that everyone eats in a healthy manner (e.g., vitamins, a balanced diet, etc.). Caregiving is what we do as mothers; it is part of our job description. Someone could give you a laundry list of things to teach or encourage your son to do but if you don't understand their importance (or more importantly if you do not demonstrate them yourself), your efforts can and will be diminished.

The guidelines presented in this chapter are purposefully general in context, because it would be virtually impossible to personalize them. If, as you read the information, you feel inspired to change your current health regimen, you should consult with a fitness or medical professional who is knowledgeable about nutrition (e.g., a registered dietician), especially if the changes you are contemplating in your diet are dramatic.

Personally, I began studying nutrition in earnest about a decade ago. Crisis is always a harbinger to change, and my crises manifested themselves in the form of chronic fatigue syndrome. I have compiled the information contained in this chapter over the past 10 years. Dr. Tom House, who has a terminal degree in exercise physiology, helped me refine the information that I had at my disposal for my son's athletic needs.[1] Over the years, I have come to value and understand the important role that whole foods and proper supplementation can play in maintaining good health.

Whenever possible, I have done my best to reference my sources for relevant points made in this chapter. By the same token, there are other reliable resources for sound nutritional information that are available on the Internet, at the library, and in bookstores if you choose to do your own research. Because your family's health, as well as your own, is something well worth investing in, you are encouraged to become as knowledgeable as possible with regard to what constitutes sound nutritional practices.

1. Much of the information in this chapter concerning nutrition and athletics is based on materials from a course I had the opportunity to take several years ago from Absolute Performance Group.

Redefining Food and Diet

The word "diet" does not mean to "lose weight," although that is the definition by which it has come to be known. In reality, the word "diet" defines the food we eat—the meals we usually consume. Your family may have a diet comprised primarily of high fiber, fruit, vegetables, and lean protein or a diet that features fats, sugars, caffeine, salt, and processed food. Most of us live in a world somewhere between the two. Your diet has developed over time; more than likely, it is based upon your culture, your beliefs about food, the tastes you grew up with, and the society in which you live. Rarely is it based upon sound nutrition.

What the majority of your diet consists of is critical to your good health. A sound diet can make the difference between having a pleasant or unpleasant experience as a person ages. Not all disease can be cured with diet, but a proper diet can improve your ability to fight off or manage disease. More importantly, diet can play a key role in having a healthy, strong body. For your son, this information can be especially critical during his athletic career. One of the primary benefits of your son learning the importance of consuming a healthy diet at a relatively young age is that not only will he carry this information with him through his sports years but also throughout his life. When I first met Tom House and he was expounding on the importance of nutrition to the group of baseball players with whom he was working, it was an easy "plate" for me to eat from (forgive the all-too-obvious pun).

Supersize It

In 2004, the movie, *Super Size Me, a Film of Epic Portions*, was released, a film which subsequently was nominated for an Academy Award. In it, filmmaker Morgan Spurlock examined the effects that the fast-food industry has had on our nation. His research yielded the following facts (you are encouraged to visit his website at www.supersizeme.com):

- French fries are the most eaten vegetable in America.
- You would have to walk for seven hours straight to burn off the calories in an order of super-sized Coke, fries, and a Big Mac.
- Sixty percent of all Americans are either overweight or obese.
- One in every three children born in the year 2000 will develop diabetes in his or her lifetime.
- Diabetes can cut 17-to-27 years off of your life.
- Most nutritionists recommend not eating fast food more than once a month.

Our kids, when they are children, learn to eat the most nutritionally-empty outrageous "foods"—sugared cereals, soda pop, doughnuts, greasy fast foods (lots and lots of fast food), and processed foods that are loaded with chemicals and empty calories. In today's world, vegetables, fruits, and whole foods have taken a backstage to the hurry-up, want-it immediately, fat-laden foods. If you add processed foods, chemically treated foods, and foods that aren't foods (like candy bars or any of the "foods" mentioned in the beginning of this paragraph), you have a national crisis on your hands. Most of us think that eating is a way to eliminate hunger. I used to think that way, but no longer.

Filling Your Personal Gas Tank

Don't you just love to eat? There is nothing equal to a plate decorated with your favorite food; the aromas and colors filling your senses; the tastes and flavors satisfying your palate and your stomach. Food is perhaps one of the most sensuous experiences of our life. But don't be fooled…food is fuel…and as much as we want to believe that it is for our sensory pleasure, it is not. The sensory enjoyment of food evolved over time through the various developmental stages of cooking and food preparation.

Our body depends upon our good judgment to provide it with the kind of fuel that will help it heal, work, think, play, move, and live. Such a role has never been truer than it currently is for our athletic sons. A time once existed when baseball players were considered the most under-conditioned athletes in the world of sports. This perception is no longer true. While a complete, well-rounded physical-training program is a necessary (and critical) element in the development of our sons as athletes, adhering to a nutritional diet is just as important to their health and well-being as is their workout regimen. In fact, without good nutrition, our sons will not have the foundation that they need when they place demands on their bodies during the course of both training and competition.

How Food Works

Once you begin chewing foods, enzymes in your mouth begin breaking the food down immediately. These enzymes send messages to your stomach that food is on the way. Have you ever chewed a piece of gum and found yourself hungry not too long after you began chewing it? That's because chewing gum signaled your stomach that food is on the way, and your stomach began creating acid to help break down the soon-to-arrive food. If you have ever experienced a stomachache after you began chewing a piece of gum, in all likelihood, your stomach was empty at the time.

Once the food reaches your stomach, it needs to break down chemically, so the body can absorb its unique vitamins, minerals, and nutrients. The stomach really does not care if the food is gourmet, how it tastes, or whether it comes with extra crème sauce. All your stomach is seeking from the food you consume is assistance to help with its digestion and fuel to feed the cells within your body.

At this point, the "what's-happening-to-the-food-you-ate" scenario gets somewhat tricky. If the food is processed, deep-fried, or overcooked, it arrives at your body's doorstep empty-handed. It's not unlike having a relative or friend show up at your doorstep with no money, expecting that you will pay for their stay and maybe even give them (without regard to value) your personal possessions to keep for their own. These empty foods are like those unwanted guests. They arrive bringing few nutrients and little-to-no enzymes to help the body's natural enzymes break them down. The body must then "steal" essential minerals, vitamins, and nutrients from other parts of your body in order to process these foods.

While your stomach may be full, your body is starving...*literally*. Foods that are nutritionally empty and lacking in enzyme activity take longer to break down in your stomach and can result in a myriad of problems, such as acid indigestion or irritable bowel syndrome, to name just a few. They can also result in undigested food particles entering your colon, thereby leading to other poor health factors that, over time, can impact your health in a more serious way.

The Importance of Hydration

To quote a newspaper article by Paula Story that appeared in the *San Diego Union* (August 30, 2005; Currents section) entitled, *Fluid Situation; Soak Up Information About Simple, Life-Giving Water*:

> "Mom was right. Our bodies use water to regulate temperature, carry oxygen and nutrients to our cells, remove waste, cushion joints, protect organs and tissues, and assist in nearly every major function. Even mild dehydration—one percent or two percent of your body weight—can make you tired or lethargic and trigger headaches, *muscle weakness*, or *dizziness*, according to Mayo Foundation for Medical Education and Research."(Emphasis added)

As you can see, maintaining fluid levels can be critical to a person's health. This factor is never truer than when it comes to an athlete, especially when competing in heat. Since our bodies are made up of 55-to-60 percent water (women and men, respectively), it only makes sense that we must keep our fluid levels up. Coaches who withhold water as a means of making their players "tough" need to rethink their extremely misinformed opinions on this issue.

The number and variety of sports drinks currently on the market are plentiful and are actually giving some soft-drink manufacturers a run for their money. However, many of these drinks are also very high in sugar content. Accordingly, if you are concerned with your son's sugar intake, it is essential that you read the labels on them. Another thirst-quenching option is to purchase water that has been enhanced with electrolytes, which, all factors considered, makes it a more desirable choice. Whatever you do, just make sure your son is properly hydrated when it comes time for him to practice, work out, or play in a game.

Snacking It Up

When providing snacks at or between games, snacks lower in processed sugar are recommended. While carbohydrates are important for athletes to maintain high levels of energy, it is important to also include an appropriate amount of protein. (Note: Most registered dieticians suggest that a person should consume approximately 22 percent of their daily caloric intake in the form of protein). Seeds, nuts, fruits, and low sugar energy bars are always a good source of protein. Candy bars, while a favorite of almost every young athlete who ever played the game, are not a sound nutritional option. Accordingly, if you do purchase candy as a snack for your son, just make sure you balance it with other more healthy choices, such as nuts or sunflower seeds.

Macronutrients and Micronutrients

We consume macronutrients every day in the form of proteins, carbohydrates, and fats. These elements supply the body with calories. Macronutrients also provide, within their individual structure, components that determine and influence our physiology and metabolism.

Micronutrients, on the other hand, entail the vitamins, minerals, antioxidants, and various phytonutrients (plant chemicals) that are hidden in macronutrients. While individual vitamins are helpful, most times they require complementary "buddies" to be assimilated into the body. Getting these micronutrients from whole or wild-grown foods (also known as green foods) is always the best option. However, with the mass processing of foods that currently exists in the marketplace, many individuals feel that supplements have become a necessary way of life.

If you decide to purchase supplements, if at all possible, you should find a reputable health-food store or supplier. Many (if not all) of these stores have an employee who is quite knowledgeable about vitamins who can help guide you toward the products that will best fit your pocketbook and your perceived supplement needs. You should keep in mind that store brands are often, if not always, just as good as the name brands.

A Diet for All Seasons—On and Off the Diamond

The appendices of this book include a shopping list of the supplements that I believe are essential for your son's well-being. Keep in mind, however, that this list of supplements is a general guideline and should not be regarded as a personalized prescription for you. Like all general observations, it is important to tailor these particular recommendations to your son's personal physical traits (size and weight), likes and dislikes, level of fitness, eating patterns, and your opinions on his supplement needs. Because you know your son better than anyone else, you will be in the best position to know what you feel he needs with regard to supplements and what your budget can afford. In reality, supplements can be expensive. In my opinion, the most important supplements for everyone, regardless of age, are multiple vitamins, probiotics, and enzymes.

It should be noted that some of the following listed supplements are only suitable for *older* players (high school juniors and older). Wherever appropriate, this factor has been noted at the end of the description for the vitamin. In those instances when the age of the person taking the supplement is not an issue, the indication "for all players" is included. This list can also be employed as a resource guide if you do your own research on supplementation.

■ *Multiple Vitamins.* In the case of your son, I recommend that you find a good multiple vitamin that is designed for males. You should avoid most chewable candy-coated multiple vitamins unless recommended by a health/fitness professional, naturopath, or nutritionist. Most health stores can tell you what dose and brands will work for your son's age, height, and weight. *(For all players.)*

■ *Vitamin C.* The average male body is made up of 60 percent water, with a 10 percent variance either way, depending upon the person's fat content. Vitamin C is an antioxidant that protects the watery parts of your body. Antioxidants basically destroy free radicals (oxygen gone amuck) that, over time, will break down your body, contributing to aging and disease. According to *The Nutrition Desk Reference*, vitamin C "plays a major role in collagen formation." Collagen is a protein that forms the basis for connective tissue, one of the most important tissues in the body. "It binds muscle cells together, gives support, and maintains shape in intervertebral disks…and provides movement to joints." In addition, vitamin C can assist the body in dealing with stress effectively.

Vitamin C can be found in whole foods, such as fruits and vegetables, especially citrus, green peppers, fresh dark green leafy vegetables, broccoli, cantaloupe, and strawberries. If your son avoids fruits and vegetables, I recommend that you provide him with an Ester-C vitamin (a vitamin that assimilates more readily than a standard C vitamin and tends to be less upsetting to the stomach). A person can consume as much as 5,000 milligrams of vitamin C a day. Personally, I suggest starting slowly with his vitamin C intake and building to an appropriate dose. *(For all players.)*

■ *CoQ10.* In my opinion, CoQ10 may well be one of the most remarkable supplements in existence. CoQ10 is a powerful antioxidant that provides the cells with energy, enabling the body to better heal and regenerate itself. The mitochondria acts as the powerhouse of the cell, breaking down sugar that releases energy required for cellular function. One unique fact that you may find interesting is that everyone's mitochondria is derived from their mother.

Our liver produces CoQ10, but the body's production wanes with age. Some foods, such as sardines, broccoli, spinach, and peanuts, carry CoQ10 in their biological structure. However, because CoQ10 is fragile and easily destroyed in cooking or food processing, supplements are a more reliable source of this substance. When shopping for CoQ10, if possible, you should purchase it suspended in oil, such as flaxseed or vitamin E oil. It is a costly supplement, but well worth the investment, in my opinion. *(For older players only.)*

■ *Omega-3, 6, and 9 Oil.* Otherwise known as essential fatty acids, omega oils have a vitally important role in your health and well-being. These oils can be found in flaxseed, fish, eggs, some nuts, some grains, and avocados, just to name a few sources for them. If you decide to augment your son's diet with these oils, I recommend that you use a high-quality gel capsule that is a compilation of flax, sunflower and sesame oil, cold pressed and unrefined. Such a capsule can provide appropriate proportions of omega-3, 6, and 9 oils.

Because essential fatty acids cannot be produced by the body, they must be obtained in foodstuffs you consume. Omega oils support the immune and nervous systems of your body, as well as your cardiovascular and reproductive systems. The human body requires these fatty acids to repair cell membranes. They also help prepare the cells of the body to receive nutrition and expel waste products. More importantly, essential fatty acids can help athletes by preventing inflammation, supporting the immune system, and producing healthy skin. When the body is fighting to maintain homeostasis, it needs all the assistance it can get.

Without going into an extensive and somewhat tedious explanation of this particular supplement, I encourage you to simply consider these oils as lubricants for the body. While the American diet is relatively abundant in omega-9 fats (butter and animal fats) and partially sufficient in omega-6 fats (such as corn/olive oil), it is relatively low, to the point of being absent in omega-3 oil (unless your family dines regularly on deepwater fish). The key point to be emphasized is that taking these supplements can support our body in many ways, in my opinion, from the heart to the head. For a more thorough explanation of how fatty acids work, you are encouraged to visit www.goodfats.pamrotella.com. *(For all players; a teaspoon of flaxseed oil a day can be substituted.)*

■ *Glucosamine and Chondroitin.* Both glucosamine and chondroitin are present in our bodies naturally and contribute to the health of cartilage. In my opinion, it can be very beneficial for baseball players to supplement their diet with these products, primarily because the repetitive motions that are often required in baseball can weaken the cartilage that surrounds and protects the body's joints. Research has shown that augmenting the diet with these supplements can lead to articular cartilage repair and, in some cases, offer more relief from inflammation than ibuprofen. Evidence also exists that glucosamine and chondroitin can help increase function and flexibility in the joints. *(For older players only.)*

■ *Food Enzymes.* Being on the run and depending upon fast food can be a huge handicap for athletes, because most of the food consumed in these circumstances is devoid of vitamins, minerals, and enzymes, but high in fat, sugar, and preservatives that can tax the body heavily. In my opinion, food enzymes, given the dietary limitations that currently exist in our society, may be one of the most important supplements that you can take.

If you decide to augment your son's diet with enzymes, it is important that he take enzyme supplements that have a complex composition. In that regard, the supplements he consumes should include at least the following elements: amylase (breaks down starch), protease (breaks down protein), lipase (breaks down fat and fat soluble vitamins), and lactase (breaks down dairy). The enzymes I consume are even more complex, containing glucoamylase (breaks down carbohydrates), invertase (splits sucrose into glucose and fructose), peptidase (reduces inflammation), phytase (improves phosphorous utilization in soybean meal), and cellulase (breaks down cellulose or fiber).

Enzymes are a critical link to life; your body produces them…but not all of them. Nothing in the body really works without them—kind of like your home when you are away from your family. *(For all players.)*

■ *Probiotics.* Healthy intestinal function is critical to the health and well-being of every individual. You undoubtedly have heard of "anti" biotics; well, these are "pro" biotics. When you think of "pro," you think of the best, you think of being on the same side of something, you think of good. That is what "probiotics" are—they are good for your body. They replant the "good" bacteria into your colon that are essential for protecting you from disease and assisting you with the elimination of waste and poisons from your body. An unhealthy colon can manifest itself in many forms, including allergies, headaches, lack of energy, excessive fatigue, digestive disorders, and mood swings.

If your son was on antibiotics as a child (most children took them for everything from colds to strep to ear infections and a thousand other childhood ailments), a strong likelihood exists, in my opinion, that your son not only needs probiotics *for* his well-being but requires them to help *reestablish* his well-being. Without a healthy colon, nutrients can have a very hard time making their way to their destination. The wall of a colon must be clean for nutrients to penetrate properly. A significant amount of research exists that indicates there is a direct correlation between the visceral senses in your body and your brain.

The best probiotic supplements can be found in the refrigerator section of a health food store. In that regard, I recommend a combination of acidophilus (for the large intestine) and bifidus (for the small intestine). As the saying goes, "the best offense is a good defense." As such, probiotics can help establish a strong defense system against illness in your son's body. *(For all ages.)*

■ *Green Foods.* Currently, a number of available sources exist for "green foods." Often referred to as "wild grown" foods, green foods include such items as blue green algae, spirulina, and chlorella, to name just a few. High in chlorophyll, green foods provide important nutrients that are absent in a typically normal, everyday diet. Over time, the soil has been depleted of minerals and nutrients. This unfortunate occurrence has resulted in food having less nutrition at the present time than even 20 years ago. Because lakes and oceans do not suffer the same depletion as the soil, the food that comes from these sources is generally higher in nutrition. In my opinion, taking a green foods supplement can support your body in a way that will make you stand up and take notice. *(For all ages.)*

■ *Protein Powders.* If you decide to increase your son's consumption of protein with a supplement, I recommend using protein powders that are without sugar additives. In this regard, my personal favorite is Jay Robb, a brand that is available on both the west and east coasts. If you are unable to find this brand locally, you can search on the Internet for a distributor. *Show Me the Way* is another brand of protein supplements that sweetens with stevia. Whatever brand of protein supplements you ultimately decide to purchase for your son, you should do your best to avoid additives. *(For all ages.)*

Foodstuffs to Avoid

The following list of foodstuffs to avoid may seem somewhat short. I am sure I could have written a whole book on things you should avoid. In the first place, it is not my intention to take all the fun out of food for you, and secondly, I believe that the items on the following list (albeit short), are important enough to bring to your attention. None of the things listed are "bad," unless over-consumed. In that regard, Aristotle's counsel of "moderation in all things" is as applicable today as it was more than two thousand years ago when he shared his thoughts with the world.

■ *Preservatives.* Preservatives kill natural enzymes and make food last longer. Anything that is "natural" has within its composition natural-occurring enzymes that break it down, making it decompose. This process is simply the cycle of life. Food distributors ostensibly use preservatives to keep our food safe. A more likely reason, however, is the fact that preservatives can extend the shelf life of foodstuffs. When a loaf of bread lasts longer than your suntan lotion, you know that you have not made a good food choice.

Clarity and mental acuity are as critical to the game of baseball as being able to hit the ball or throw a good pitch. If your son is young and you have control over his diet (as I expect you do), I highly recommend that you empty your cupboards of processed foods that contain preservatives, like BHT, MSG, sodium nitrates, and BHQT, to name just a few. Preservatives pass through the blood/brain barrier and can cause havoc with a person's thinking process, creating distractions and what most would call "antsy" behavior. For more information on this subject, you should visit www.feingold.org. To the extent possible, I strongly recommend that you encourage your son, not by coercion, but through education, example, and persuasion, to make as many "good" choices as he can when he chooses which food to eat.

In my mind, it is impossible and unreasonable for any mother (me included) to believe that their sons will be perfect in any respect, let alone with their diets. If, for any reason, you feel eliminating foods that contain preservatives from your cupboard is too daunting an undertaking, you should do your best to at least moderate your son's intake of them.

■ *Aspartame*. Aspartame is a synthetic chemical additive made of three "natural" ingredients (two amino acids: phenylalanine and aspartic acid), as well as methyl alcohol (also known as methanol), a substance that can have an unnatural affect on your body. Several compelling studies have been conducted that indicate that this product can have negative side effects on some people. Moderation in all things is important, but, for the most part, elements that are not natural make it more difficult, if not impossible, for your cells to assimilate the essential nutrients in foodstuffs.

If you want to sweeten something your son consumes, you should consider alternative sweeteners such as stevia, which is derived from a Brazilian shrub, stevia rebaudiana. Because it is a highly concentrated sweetener, you will only need very little of it to produce the level of sweetness you prefer. You should also be aware that a small percentage of the population is sensitive to stevia (primarily individuals who are allergic to bees), so I would recommend testing it in small doses. Some nutritionists refer to stevia as a health food. If all else fails, consuming sugar in small doses is acceptable, as long as your son practices good dental hygiene.

■ *Alcohol*. Alcohol crosses the blood/brain barrier and alters an individual's moods. Fortunately, many people have no desire to drink. On the other hand, many do. If your son is a t-ball player at the tender age of six, I can only imagine you must be thinking, "why is this information on alcohol included in this book?" The truth is, your son will grow up and be pressured by his peers to drink. How you personally treat alcohol in your lifestyle can greatly influence his decisions in this regard. Accordingly, you should never forget that the life you lead will be the mirror that reflects the example he will follow.

The numerous reasons why you would want your son to avoid alcohol consumption are as clear and valid as they can be. Most people are aware of the dangers of addiction to alcohol, the derailment from responsibility that consuming alcohol can induce, and perhaps the most frightening factor of all...the perils associated with drunk driving. Athletes have an even more compelling reason to reconsider the case against consuming alcohol—the impact that drinking can have on their musculoskeletal system. Perhaps, you may have noticed these side effects if you have tried to do something physically demanding after a night of celebration.

Simply stated, your muscles do not like the affects of alcohol. When a person exercises, he is literally breaking down the tissue in his body and rebuilding it. Nutrients will help the healing, rebuilding, and strengthening of muscle tissue after a hard workout. For each 12-ounce beer or one-ounce shot of alcohol, your muscles take two days to recover. An athlete is placing himself in a physiological deficit when he drinks. Accordingly, if you want to help your son make smart decisions concerning alcohol consumption and its potential impact on his baseball journey, you must teach him what he should know about this intoxicating beverage.

Your son must have a healthy body if he is to perform at a high, competitive level. In my case, I basically healed myself using nutrition as my blueprint. As such, I can tell you from personal experience that I have found numerous benefits in eating properly and augmenting my diet with supplements. While each one of us is unique, we are all (in many ways) the same. Giving yourself permission to explore nutritional alternatives may open up a whole new world for you. In this regard, you should ask your health/fitness professional what might work best for you, your son, and other members of your family. When I started to investigate the possible role that supplements could play in my life, I found very little support through traditional medicine and medical channels. Fortunately, in recent years, it seems to me that more and more physicians are looking to complement their patients' treatments with targeted supplementation. Obviously, if that is indeed the situation, it's about time.

Properly nurturing your son with food is yet another of the seemingly endless list of responsibilities that you have as a loving, caring mother. Such a step may require that you assume several roles—advocate, educator, role model, and responsible parent, to name just a few. All of these roles will be appropriate at one time or another and well worth the effort. In the end, the process may also change your life for the better.

16

Enhancement Enchantment

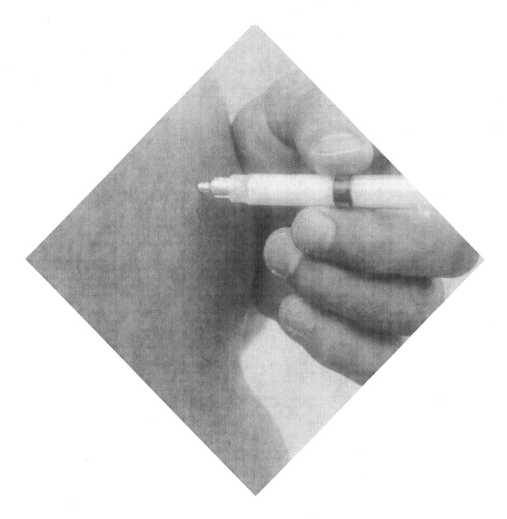

"…and they lived happily ever after…"

— Fairytale endings

Enchantment comes from the word "enchant" meaning "to influence by charms and incantation; synonym: bewitch." Enhancement comes from the word "enhance" meaning "to make greater (as in value, desirability or attractiveness); synonym: heighten." Combine the two words "enhancement" and "enchantment", and you have "en*chance*ment". When the two ideas are mixed together and action is taken based upon these two principles, people end up taking high-risk *chances* with their lives—not immediately perhaps, but definitely with their future. As a mother, you need to know why.

Chief Cook and Bottle Washer

We nurture. That is what mothers do. What we don't always do is teach our kids the reality of what happens to our bodies when we put things into it that don't belong. The media promote misunderstandings about many, many things, especially drug use. No one can legitimately question the fact that there are many important and quite useful drugs on the market today that save lives. However, the misuse and abuse of drug consumption in this country is at an epidemic level. You cannot turn on the television or even go to the movies without drug advertisements being shoved down your throat. In fact, these advertisements do not even tell you what some of the drugs are for; they simply suggest that you ask your doctor if you need to take their drug of choice, whatever that is. They treat the ingestion of drugs into the body as if it were as natural as eating an apple.

We are also at the mercy of a "microwave" society. We want everything yesterday, whether it is a hamburger or a perfect body. No one really wants to do what our ancestors did, which was to patiently focus on and work toward a specific goal, all the while knowing that every sensible action we undertake can help lead us forward in our lives. No, we want it now. No, wait, we want it yesterday.

Drug abuse is a subject about which I am very passionate. Drug abuse is destroying the very fabric of the lives of people everywhere. It does not matter whether drugs come in the form of cigarettes, chewing tobacco, alcohol, marijuana, or substances like anabolic steroids. The fundamental truth about drugs is that they "*enchance*" people into believing untruths, while destroying both their bodies and their lives. Drugs make false promises of happiness, wealth, fame, or, at the very least, an escape from the pressures of our lives. But, it's all temporary. They promise a quick fix that will fool us into believing, at least for the moment, that life will be good if we are just stronger, faster, more relaxed, not as uptight, less anxious...and the list goes on and on.

Why would anyone allow themselves to be seduced by the empty promises of drugs? For enhancement, pure and simple. If taking a pill would make you five foot eight and 140 pounds of pure muscle and beauty, would you be tempted? Your response would be further tempted by the promise of more money than you've ever had in your life. Get the point? In reality, it's a question of what you want, when you want it, and what is reasonably (and safely) within reach.

The older your son is and the more he pushes himself up the ranks of the baseball ladder, the more the promise of material factors, such as scholarships and big money, are like aphrodisiacs. Too many young men believe they will never enter the "land of milk, honey, and baseball" without anabolic steroids. Nicotine calms their nerves. If they are lucky enough to enter the land of "milk and honey," when is enough, enough? Fame, breaking records, fan adulation…Obviously, baseball has a very serious issue on its hands.

Gary Huckabay, a writer for *Baseball Prospectus*, interviewed a team trainer on the issue of using anabolic steroids. The thoughtful answers given by the trainer who was interviewed brings some very serious issues to light. When asked how much benefit steroid use could provide to a player, his response was, "For some guys, it's the difference between making a few million bucks and staying in Double A." The trainer then went on to make an even more eye-opening comment. "Steroid use is drug abuse, just like crack, cocaine, heroin, or anything else. Stopping drug abuse of any kind is extremely difficult."

In fact, baseball is facing a very serious epidemic of steroid abuse. It is estimated that over a half million high school students are using anabolic steroids in just grades nine and 10. With their whole lives in front of them, these young students are gambling on immediate gratification over long-term fulfillment.

As a mother, I am hopeful. I am reminded of a woman by the name of Candy Lightner, who in 1980, together with a small group of mothers formed MADD, Mothers Against Drunk Drivers. There are very few people in this country who do not know what MADD stands for today. In the same way Lightner's heartbreak and passion created a national awareness about the dangers of alcohol, as mothers of athletes we have a responsibility (and opportunity) to make sure that our children become fully aware of what drugs can do to their body.

In reality, ensuring that your son doesn't get involved with drugs can be a daunting task. For example, simply demanding that your son not take drugs is rarely effective. On the other hand, there are a few potentially helpful steps that you can undertake that can be effective in this regard, including:

- You can talk to your son about drug abuse in an open, straightforward way.
- You can teach your son to love and honor his body by your example.
- You can treat your son with respect so that he conducts himself in a respectful manner—physically, mentally, and emotionally.
- You can educate your son, through written materials and online sources, regarding what happens to people who try to make drugs an answer in their lives.
- You can listen to your son when he needs to talk, without being judgmental.

- You can provide clear boundaries and guidelines concerning your son's behavior and bestow more stringent supervision of him when appropriate.
- You can engage in active, supportive, and loving parenting.

Gary Smith spoke to the heartbreaking issue of anabolic steroid use in baseball in an article he wrote for *Sports Illustrated* titled, "What Do We Do Now?" (March 20, 2005). Smith's essay came on the heels of congressional hearings on the subject, along with Jose Canseco's book, *Juiced*. (As the mother of a baseball player, I find Canseco's enthusiastic endorsement of anabolic steroids to be particularly disgusting.) Smith concluded that, in his opinion, physical enhancement for athletes will be part of our future. As he put it, "The use of anabolic steroids, in retrospect (30 years from now), will seem almost prehistoric." Furthermore, he stated that he was addressing this issue because he believed the use of steroids constituted "cheating." Steroid use involves far more than cheating at a game; the athletes who use steroids are cheating themselves out of their health and maybe even their lives.

Smith made a particularly pointed comment about what might occur in the future with regard to enhancement efforts designed to make athletes bigger, faster, and better than the average individual. He spoke of "the naturals"—athletes who are good simply because they have natural gifts and diligently train and take care of their precious bodies. "Natural" athletes treat their health and their bodies with respect. He goes on to state that it will be "mothers who want the best for their kids, that's who will break the back of the naturals."

In my opinion, Smith was referring to a mother's passion for her children (in this case her son) to succeed in life. I believe that it will be mothers who change the face of this nightmare. Hopefully, it will occur because mothers will come together in a more powerful and meaningful way. In fact, mothers *can* make a difference. Personally, I would love to see *Diamond Moms* be to drugs what MADD is to alcohol. Mother Teresa said it best:

> "Never doubt that a small group of dedicated people can make a difference. Indeed, it is the only thing that ever has."

Mothers can be a powerful, mighty force if they unite on the issue of drug and/or steroid abuse. They can force changes that will make a difference for their sons and future generations. It will all happen through awareness and education.

Respect for Our Bodies

Face it. Almost no one is harder on their bodies than women. Even those women who are in shape tend to spend an unduly amount of time beating themselves up mentally and physically. They are willing to starve themselves in an attempt to get thin. They work out until they are bone tired. They often obsess over their appearance. On the other hand, some women are hard on their bodies for the exact opposite reasons. They don't exercise regularly. They don't eat the right foods. They don't get enough sleep. All factors considered, women who live on the extreme ends of one point of view or the other rarely feel comfortable when it comes to their physical image and often struggle to find a healthy balance between taking care of themselves and others.

In truth, the way we take care of ourselves can say more to our sons about respecting (or disrespecting in some circumstances) the human body than anything we might otherwise assert. Ralph Waldo Emerson said it best when he proclaimed, "What you do speaks so loudly I cannot hear what you say."

Most women are born with bodies that are the automobile equivalent of a finely tuned Lexus. For the most part, however, too many of us grow up and old treating and disrespecting our bodies like "rent-a-wreck" cars. You are probably wondering why the subject of enhancement drugs is being addressed in such a backdoor style.

As stated in previous chapters, children tend to learn what they live and see. As such, if you are willing to put harmful things into your body or treat it disrespectfully, then your sons will be sent a message that such behavior is acceptable. He will be given the mistaken impression that the human body is infallible and can take unlimited amounts of abuse without undue consequences. He will also be exposed to the concept that the "end justifies the means" (i.e., it is alright to do whatever is necessary if in the end he gets what he wants). In reality, a person's actions do have consequences. Far too often, young athletes are either not aware of the probable outcomes of their activities or simply don't care. Too many individuals simply cannot imagine being in ill health when they are strong, strapping, physically active athletes. The key point in this regard is that you should take a serious look at your convictions and lifestyle and ask yourself a very important question, "What am I saying to my son when I am saying nothing at all?"

When Juice Isn't Juice

Anabolic steroid is the common term for a synthetic substance related to the male sex hormone testosterone. The use of anabolic steroids can result in a number of significant changes in the human body, including enhancing the growth of skeletal muscle and increasing the development of male sexual characteristics. While anabolic steroids were developed in the 1930s to treat delayed development of puberty and some types of impotence, in recent years, they have been used to help treat HIV patients.

The level of anabolic steroid use exploded in the 1960s when body-builders began using them to enhance muscle size and strength. For years, most people considered them legal. At the very least, their use was ignored by athletic organizations that governed drug abuse. Over time, as their harmful side effects became more well-known, various federal agencies passed legislation outlawing their possession and their use. At the present time, they are available in the United States only if a qualified attending physician prescribes them. For example, the commonly prescribed medication prednisone is a steroid. All major sports governing bodies in the United States (amateur, as well as professional), including the NCAA, have declared anabolic steroid use to be illegal and impose penalties on any player caught using them. The NCAA mandates that multiple violations of steroid use can result in a player being banned from collegiate ball. Even Major League Baseball, as of late 2005, has finally taken an aggressive stand regarding the use of anabolic steroids by professional baseball players. Players face an escalating series of suspensions if they test positive for steroid use. (Welcome to the 21st century Donald Fehr, however reluctant he seems to have been to address such a serious health issue.)

Why Anabolic Steroids Are Harmful

Anabolic steroids have long been a subject of debate. Years ago, an article appeared in *Sports Illustrated* about Lyle Alzado, an Oakland Raiders football player. He appeared on the magazine's cover, the first poster child for arguments against these insidious substances. Alzado admittedly used anabolic steroids while playing with the Raiders and eventually died from a brain tumor in 1992, a tumor he attributed to his abuse/use of steroids.

The chapter on nutrition in this book provides a brief overview of how food and other factors can affect your physical well-being. The potential impact of steroid use on your health is much more serious, as the following list of the major side effects of what anabolic steroids can do to the human body vividly illustrates:

■ *Heightened risk of injury.* Individuals who increase their level of muscular strength and size by taking anabolic steroids may be exposed to an elevated risk of injuring their tendons and ligaments. Such a risk is caused, in part, by the fact that muscle tissue strengthens faster than connective tissue, and, to a degree, the tendons and ligaments can not accommodate quickly enough.

■ *Unbecoming conduct.* Steroid use has been linked to increased levels of aggressive behavior. The extent of the impact that steroids have on an individual's mood and actions depends on the number of factors, including the type of anabolic steroids used, the size and frequency of the steroids doses, how long a person takes steroids, and how a person takes steroids (e.g., orally or by injection).

■ *Increased potential for heart disease.* Research has found that steroid use raises the cholesterol level in an individual's blood. Oral anabolic steroids have been shown to dramatically decrease the level of HDL-C (the "good" cholesterol) and increase the level of LDL-C (the "bad" cholesterol) in the blood, thereby substantially raising a person's risk of coronary heart disease.

■ *Beleaguered complexion.* Individuals who use steroids frequently suffer from acne.

Steroids can cause an individual's oil glands to enlarge and secrete more frequently. In turn, the excess secretion can clog the pores of the skin, resulting in unsightly changes in a steroid user's complexion.

■ *Blood clots.* Steroids can cause the platelets in the blood to be more likely to stick together. By increasing the likelihood for the formation of blood clots, steroids increase a person's chances of having a heart attack resulting from a blood clot in the coronary arteries.

■ *Arrested development.* Adolescents who take steroids can experience premature closure of the epiphyscal (growth) plates. As such, taking steroids can cause children to have stunted growth.

■ *Liver toxicity.* Because the liver is the principle site for steroid clearance for individuals who take anabolic steroids orally, an excessive intake of steroids can be toxic to the liver. As a result, the liver can become vulnerable to serious damage, such as cysts and tumors. This damage can develop relatively rapidly after a person consumes a substantial amount of steroids, or it may develop gradually over a period of years as a result of prolonged consumption of small amounts of potentially toxic substances, such as steroids.

■ *Hair today, gone tomorrow.* Steroids use may result in hair loss. For example, men prone to baldness may lose their hair faster. Concurrently (or separately), steroid users may also experience an increase in their level of body hair (in areas other than on their scalp).

■ *Reproduction.* Long-term anabolic steroid abuse has been associated with a negative impact upon the male reproductive system. It has been known to lower the production of sperm and reduce the level of several essential reproductive hormones.

■ *Masculinizing effects.* For those Diamond Moms who also have daughters, it is important to be aware of the fact that, similar to their male counterparts, steroids have also been shown to have serious side effects for women. For example, depending upon the frequency of use and dosage levels, taking steroids will cause most women to exhibit an enhanced level of male characteristics, including a deepening of the voice, an increase in the amount of facial hair, and the development of a more "manly" body shape. In addition, steroids can cause a woman's breasts to shrink and her menstrual cycle to be disrupted. In men, however, steroids can have a feminizing effect (e.g., the development of breast-like tissue).

Stopping Anabolic Steroid Use

Like any drug or chemical that is brought into the human body on a regular basis when it doesn't belong there, discontinuing its use can lead to a variety of withdrawal symptoms—some more serious than others. Without question, one of the most dangerous withdrawal symptoms that can occur is depression, which although serious in its own right, can lead to suicide attempts in some circumstances. In that regard, a recent article in the *San Diego Union* newspaper disclosed that males are four times as likely to commit suicide as females. While this study was not in any way linked to the use of anabolic steroids, the information it provided certainly can be relevant to the parents of young athletes. Disappointments taken to extremes when drugs unduly influence a passionate and impressionable young man can lead to outcomes of which parental nightmares are made. Unfortunately, the symptoms associated with depression can be long-term, lasting for as much as a year after the use of the drug has ceased. As such, the parents of a young athlete suffering from depression wake up to a very unstable, frightening set of circumstances every morning.

What Can You Do?

Educate, educate, communicate, communicate, educate, communicate…Be a family, eat together, play together, laugh together, cry together. Teach each other. The National Institute on Drug Abuse (NIDA), part of the National Institute of Health, recommends presenting both the benefits and risks when talking to your kids about drug abuse. These experts have found this approach to be more effective and beneficial than simply addressing (or attacking) the issue out of fear. Your son will find you more credible if you can present the information in a less biased way, stating the benefits (such as calmer nerves in the case of tobacco or increased muscle size in the case of steroids) and then detailing the potential side effects and long-term effects. It is important that you approach this situation from an informed position, rather than a fearful place.

Talk to your son about how strength training, core work, stretching, and proper nutrition can take his body to its optimum performance level. This step can be done at any age; in fact, the earlier the better (as long as his conditioning program is based on sound principles). As your son ages, if you can, you should get a qualified professional trainer for him so he has proper instruction in conditioning and strength training. If, for any reason, you cannot obtain a personal trainer, both the library and the Web offer a variety of potentially helpful resources on the subjects. NIDA recognizes and encourages a multicomponent, team-centered approach when it comes to conditioning and workout programs. If your son's team is not engaged in such a program, you should consider going to the gym with him or encourage his dad to go. Studies have found that this kind of approach can reduce steroid abuse by at lest 50 percent (or more).

Chewing Tobacco and Baseball

You may be wondering what "enhancement" has to do with tobacco. It appears that those kids who use chewing tobacco start chewing it either because they think it is "cool" or because older players are using it. At some level, these individuals believe that chewing tobacco "enhances" their image. In a few instances, players believe that because the use of chewing tobacco calms their nerves, it "enhances" their moods by eliminating emotional tension. All of the probable "reasons" concerning why baseball players use chewing tobacco are further compounded with the fact that chewing tobacco is part of the tradition of baseball, much in the same way that hot dogs, popcorn, peanuts, and sunflower seeds are. Surprisingly, at some level, players believe the use of chewing tobacco "enhances" the tradition of the sport. Such an attitude is another unfortunate example of the "when in Rome do as the Romans do" mentality.

Traditions are hard to overcome, however. Most are cherished; leaving memories that will warm our hearts in our old age. Baseball is not only full of traditions…it *is* a tradition. Unfortunately, on occasion, some components of these "traditions" can be unhealthy or harmful.

Everyone knows that smoking tobacco is bad for you. Few individuals, however, are aware of the fact that the "dipping," "chewing," "spitting" kind of tobacco, the kind that is messy, is just as lethal, if not more so. Chewing tobacco is prevalent among males from middle-school age to adults. An estimated 7.7 million Americans, almost all male, use smokeless tobacco. Combine an all-male sport with this statistic, and you can see the odds of your son chewing increase substantially. Chewing tobacco is infiltrating the baseball diamonds of America—not the dirt diamonds but the human diamonds, those gems we call our sons.

The Modern Spittoon Squad

There are two types of smokeless tobacco in the United States. Chewing tobacco comes in the form of loose leaves, while snuff (the other kind) is finely ground tobacco that can be dry, moist, or in sachets (like tea bags). For the most part, this type of tobacco is "dipped" from a can between the fingers and placed between the lower lip and gum, allowing the nicotine to penetrate into the bloodstream via the mucous membranes in the mouth.

Not only do our mouths provide a direct path into our stomachs, they also offer a direct route to our bloodstream. That is why a nitroglycerin pill (a drug used to bring relief from the pain and pressure of angina) is placed under the tongue of a heart patient. It immediately enters the bloodstream, relaxing the smooth muscles of the body, such as those that are found in the heart and blood vessels. In the same way, when tobacco is placed along the lining of the mouth, nicotine is allowed to enter the bloodstream just as efficiently, but with the opposite effect. It constricts the blood vessels and poisons the body.

Smokeless tobacco contains nicotine, a stimulant and addictive ingredient. When it is combined with chewing tobacco and taken into the body via the mouth, it delivers a higher nicotine level to the body than smoking a cigarette. The nicotine delivered in chewing tobacco is retained in the bloodstream for a longer period of time than when a person smokes a cigarette. The mucous membrane of the mouth quickly absorbs the nicotine, creating a "buzz." In fact, smokeless tobacco has been found to be as addictive as cocaine or heroin. Over time, the addiction is embedded more deeply into the body, making it harder and harder to give up the habit.

To make matters worse, tobacco companies do all that they can to make chewing tobacco more inviting to young males. For example, they flavor the tobacco so it tastes good and place it near candy in convenience stores, making it easy for kids to see, if not buy. Sugar, coconut, strawberry, and mint flavors disguise and ease youngsters into the habit of "chewing" at a relatively early age, while hooking these young men to a life of addiction. The coarseness of the tobacco leaf cuts and chaffs the inside of the mouth, increasing the speed with which the nicotine is absorbed into the bloodstream.

Harmful Side Effects

Nicotine is a drug, legal though it may be. It causes increased heart rates and high blood pressure, constricts the flow of blood in the arteries, compromises the immune system, and increases the risk of blood clots forming, while decreasing peripheral circulation. Nicotine ingested in the form of chewing tobacco has also been found to increase the levels of blood sugar. For unknown reasons, those individuals who chew tobacco are 20 percent more likely to experience these health issues than those who smoke tobacco.[1] As can be seen, a person does not have to ingest nicotine by smoking a cigarette to be seriously harmed by it.

Chewing tobacco can also contribute to oral health problems. For example, using chewing tobacco can cause the gums to recede, leukoplakia to develop (a lesion of the soft tissue that consists of white patch or plaque that cannot be scrapped off), and teeth to rot and fall out. Such use can also cause cancerous lesions to develop, which can lead to a deformation of the face or even death in a few, isolated instances. The key point to remember is that dipping is a very serious and real danger to the youth of this country, but even more so for the boys who play baseball.

At some point (hopefully), the athlete who uses chewing tobacco will decide that enough is more than enough and stop his ill-founded habit. The "gift" that keeps on giving will give a little bit more. Nicotine withdrawal can cause several problems, including constipation, tiredness, lack of energy, nervousness, irritability, hunger, and cravings. Each can be very uncomfortable and somewhat challenging, especially when it is combined with the frequently stressful aspects of baseball.

---

1. Health Day Reporter, Randy Dotinga, Friday, June 24, 2005

What to Do

As a mother, you must educate your son to the dangers of smokeless tobacco. One helpful step in this regard is to let him view images online of what can happen to his beautiful face if he abuses his body with smokeless tobacco. While I don't usually recommend scare tactics, sometimes they can be very persuasive arguments that can help redirect your son's choices in a more positive direction. Just as you steered your children away from moving vehicles when they were learning to walk, you must be just as aggressive when it comes to your son and his possible use of drugs and alcohol. As a point of fact, chewing tobacco is a drug, a serious and potentially lethal drug, and represents a true and real danger to your son.

Another step that you can take to help reduce the level of smokeless tobacco is to pressure your legislators to pass laws that better protect all children from purchasing and using these products. Cigarette advertising has been curtailed for years, and yet chewing tobacco is treated as a harmless practice. During 2001, the five largest tobacco manufacturers spent $236.7 million on smokeless tobacco advertising and promotion.[2]

You can also try to persuade your son's high school coaches to implement and enforce campus rules relating to tobacco use. It is currently illegal in most states for anyone under the age of 18 or 19 to buy or use it, and no adult supervising your adolescent son should tolerate its use by minors. In my opinion, no responsible coach should use tobacco (in any form) in front of his players, regardless of the players' ages.

If your son is an adult who has become addicted to chewing tobacco, there are some alternatives he can pursue if *he* is truly interested in breaking himself of his dangerous habit. For example, a variety of non-nicotine chews are currently available on the market that can be gradually substituted for smokeless chewing tobacco. One popular brand is called Bacc-Off and can be ordered online. These chews can be added slowly to his smokeless tobacco, thereby gradually decreasing his level of nicotine intake. Over time, as a mother, you must be realistic about whether your son is addicted and the extent of his addiction. He may or may not be willing to admit that he has a problem that needs to be addressed. Accordingly, you must be willing to provide the support that he wants and the guidance that he needs in this situation.

In Conclusion

After you have done all you can do, you need to step away and hope that your son's good sense will prevail. While I wish I could tell you that all the coercion in the world will make a difference in such a situation, most likely, it will drive your son further into his nicotine-induced abyss.

---

2. Much of the information presented in this chapter is based on material that can be found on the website of the National Center for Chronic Disease Prevention and Health Promotion: http://www.cde.gov/tobacco/factsheets/smokelesstobacco.htm

The key point to emphasize is that you should not allow the information presented in this chapter to frighten you. All factors considered, it is better to light a candle and see what goes "bump in the night," than it is to pretend it doesn't exist. Once you have done your part by educating your son about the potential dangers inherent in abusing his body with anabolic steroids and/or nicotine, you need to let your son continue on his journey. It is important to recognize when you have done all you can. Have faith in your son and in what you have taught him. Hopefully, the love you have for your son will carry both of you through these muddy waters. One of your greatest gifts to him is the faith you demonstrate in him when you finally let go of his hand.

Extra Innings

(Epilogue)

The dilemma I now face as a creative person looms over me, like a bubble over a picture awaiting text. Have I shared everything that I can to help other mothers? Is the advice that I have provided balanced and fair? I constantly find myself thinking of other things to add to the book. Ideas float to my mind or my trusted friends and advisors keep feeding me other "ideas" that are just as or more viable than anything contained in the previous pages, items such as:

- Little girls can always play softball (and get college scholarships as a reward).

- Somebody needs to give mothers permission to tell fathers to "shut up" once in a while.

- Mothers must be balanced and fair when they have more than one child playing sports, especially if one is an all-star athlete and the other is not quite as talented.

- Baseball involves commitment at all ages. Such a commitment is especially important when boys play in high-level leagues (i.e., elite, travel, or summer teams). Planning a summer vacation that coincides with games can conflict with the schedule of those teams and create hardships for coaches and players alike. The "C" word entails an expansive concept, especially if a situation exists where a family is making sacrifices for something one parent or extended family members consider to be just a "game."

Much of life is common sense. Every day, in every way, we teach our children about life: how to *trust* it, how to *be* a part of it, how to *live* it, and how to *love* it. Truth be known, our intention as parents is to raise individuals who care deeply not only about themselves, but also about others and the world in which they live.

Whether by desire or design, all athletes are, to some degree, leaders. Their circumstances frequently cause them to step out of the ordinary into the extraordinary simply by being in the spotlight. They are willing to take chances and expose their strengths *and* their weaknesses to others when they are in the athletic arena. They frequently encounter critics at every turn (hopefully not from members of their family). As mothers, we try to teach them to be strong, confident, and responsible, from the onset of their youth to the twilight of their lives. Creating capable men, one day at a time…that is our job.

I feel a deep and profound connection to women. Perhaps, it is because I grew up in a matriarchal home. Even though the early years of my life were quite "bumpy," I learned that women are meant to be strong. I learned that women are meant to be fearless in the face of challenges and opportunities. I learned that women can do almost anything to which they put their mind. No limitations were ever placed on me in my home when I was growing up. Motherhood deepened these notions, even if at times, I was unsure of my footing. Life has taught me that being a woman is a wonderful thing.

I hope that you treasure who you are and recognize the incredible gifts you have been blessed with that you share with your family, especially with your baseball sons. If I have helped you connect those gifts in any way, then the effort to write this book has been well worth it. Finally, if baseball has captured your heart as it has mine, welcome to the world of *Diamond Moms*.

Understanding the Basics of the Game

■ *The Nitty Gritty*

Founded almost two hundred years ago by Abner Doubleday, baseball is truly America's game. Although it is currently played in over 30 countries, its roots and popularity are grounded in America. The game itself is designed to be played by two teams of nine players each on a relatively large field that has four bases. Depending upon the level of competition, the game is played over seven-to-nine innings. An inning consists of each team being on offense (at bat) for one-half of an inning and on defense (in the field) for one-half of an inning. The team that starts on offense is considered the visiting team, while the team that is in the field first is the home team.

During the half inning that a team is on offense, the members of that team bat in predetermined order against pitches thrown by the pitcher on the team in the field. The pitcher must throw the ball in a prescribed area over the plate (i.e., the strike zone). The batter attempts to hit the pitch. The batter stays at the plate and continues to try to hit until one of the following scenarios occurs: the ball is hit into fair territory (i.e., within the designated foul lines); the batter strikes out (each batter is given three strikes per at bat; a strike can be a pitch thrown in the strike zone at which the batter does not swing or a pitch in the strike zone at which the batter swings and misses); the batter receives a base on balls (i.e., a walk), which occurs when the pitcher throws him four pitches that are not in the strike zone before either of the two aforementioned scenarios happens; or the batter is hit by a pitch thrown by the pitcher.

If the ball is hit into fair territory, the nine players in the field attempt to catch the ball and put the batter "out" according to the rules of the game. An "out" can be achieved in any number of ways. The two most common ways are to catch the struck ball on the fly before it strikes the ground or to field a ball that has struck the ground and throw it to the first baseman who tags the bag before the batter can run from home plate to first base. A team is accorded three outs per half inning.

The basic objective of the game is for one team to score more runs than the other team. A run is scored when a batter hits a home run or advances around the four bases without being put out. If the hitter is able to reach first base on a batted ball that strikes the ground before the fielder is able to throw the ball to the base, he is "awarded" that base, whereupon he becomes a baserunner. In fact, he may hit the ball in such a way or such an area of the field that he is able to safely reach second base (a hit referred to as a "double") or third base (a hit called a "triple") before the next batter comes to the plate.

Once the batter becomes a baserunner, whether or not he is able to advance around the bases (and ultimately score a run) will depend on the actions on the batters who hit after him during that half inning. If they hit the ball into fair territory on the ground (and not a fly ball that is caught by the defensive team) and the baserunner is able to reach the next base without being forced out or the batter is not thrown out at first for the third out of the inning, the baserunner advances. A force out occurs when a ground ball is fielded and thrown to second base before the runner on first is able to reach second or thrown to third or home before a runner on second or third, respectively, is able to reach the next base.

The winner of the game is the team that scores the most runs within the prescribed number of innings to be played. If the home team is leading after the top half of the last inning, the game is over at that point. If the game is tied after the prescribed number of innings, the game continues an inning at a time until one team is able to outscore the other.

The game is supervised by individuals who are referred to as "umpires." As a rule, each game has two umpires, except for Major League games, which have four. One umpire assumes a position behind home plate and is primarily responsible for calling balls and strikes, as well as making calls on other aspects of the game (typically all calls at third and home). The second umpire assumes a position in the field and is responsible for making all calls on baserunners at first base, as well as additional calls at other bases and in the outfield, as prescribed. (It should be noted that on occasion, it often does not appear to some Diamond Moms that good eyesight is a prerequisite to be an umpire.)

■ *The Participants*

A baseball game involves two teams competing against each other. While the number of total players on a team's roster tends to vary from competitive level to competitive level, nine players on a team play at a time. If a player who is not currently in the game is substituted for someone who is, the player who is being replaced cannot return to the game. One of the primary responsibilities of a team's coaching staff is to ensure that their team has the players in the game at any given time who give their team the best chances for winning. It could be reasonably argued that at the youth level, this responsibility involves making sure that every child gets to play.

The team in the field typically has three outfielders (one each in left field, center field, and right field) and six players in the infield (pitcher, catcher, first base, second base, shortstop, and third base). Table A-1 illustrates the various areas of the field and the corresponding player who is positioned in that area. Each position requires a somewhat different set of skills and athletic abilities. The coach determines which players are best suited to play which position. Furthermore, the coach decides which individual will start the game at the various positions. Depending upon the coach's philosophy, the rules of the league in which the team plays, and the strategic circumstances, the coach may or may not substitute for a particular athlete in the game as play progresses.

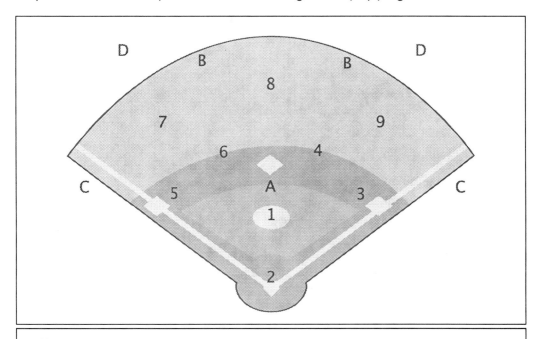

Key:

1: Pitcher
3: First base
4: Second base
5: Third base
6: Shortstop
7: Left field
8: Center
9: Right field

A: Infield
B: Outfield
C: Foul territory
D: Home run territory (FYI: designation only; not known by this name)

Table A-1. The field and the corresponding player positions

Each number is representative of a position player on a baseball diamond. These numbers are used when scoring for purposes of indicating which player(s) are involved in a particular play during a game. The table matches the number to the position of each of the nine players. The letters are simply a method used to define the various areas of the field.

■ *The Equipment Essential to the Game*

- Bats
- Balls
- Gloves
- Shoes
- Uniforms

■ *The Basic Physical Skills of the Game*

- Hitting the ball
- Fielding the ball
- Throwing the ball
- Pitching the ball
- Baserunning
- Bunting the ball

B

Baseball Lingo

This appendix offers an abbreviated list of selected baseball terms and "lingo." If you are really interested in learning more terms, you are encouraged to do your own research. One book I highly recommend is *The Language of Baseball: A Complete Dictionary of Slang Terms, Clichés, and Expressions from the Grand Ole Game*, which can be found at http://www.coacheschoice.com. I also learned on *Baseball for Dummies, 3rd Edition* as I did my own research for this appendix.

Aggressive lead. Refers to a baserunner's lead consisting of two hard shuffle steps.

Alleys. Left-center and right-center field.

Arm speed. Refers to the velocity of a pitcher's arm movement, while throwing a ball.

Arsenal. Term meaning 1) the assortment of pitches a hurler can use in a game, or 2) the offensive hitting weapons a team has at its disposal.

Assist. Term for when a player throws the ball to a teammate and his teammate records an out.

Bad hop. When a batted ball takes an unusual bounce as an infielder approaches to field it.

Balk. When a pitcher makes an illegal move, while maintaining contact with the pitcher's rubber; as a result, all base runners move up one base.

Baltimore chop. An expression used to describe when a ball is hit hard off of home plate or the hard dirt around the plate causing the ball to bounce straight up.

Banger. Term for a very close play.

Base knock. Slang term for a base hit.

Batter's box. The designated area in which a batter stands during an at bat.

Bean ball. A pitch that hits a batter.

Bench jockey. A reserve player who runs his mouth from the bench.

Bench warmer. A reserve player who plays very little.

Blooper. Term for a softly hit fly ball.

Blue darter. Slang term for a hard hit line drive.

Box score. A listing of statistics for a baseball game.

Breaking ball. A curveball or slider.

Broken bat single. When a player gets a base hit, even though he breaks his bat.

Bullpen. The area in a ballpark where the pitchers warm up on a practice mound.

Bunt. A softly tapped ball, which is supposed to go a short distance on the infield; no swing of the bat is involved.

Cannon. Term for a strong throwing arm.

Can of corn. An easy fly ball.

Caught napping. Expression for when a player is put out because he was not concentrating on the job at hand.

Change of pace. Term for a change-up pitch.

Change speeds. When a pitcher throws pitches at a variety of speeds to keep the batter off balance.

Chicken wing. Term for when a batter's front elbow is away from his rib cage area.

Chopper. A batted ball that takes several bounces, with one bounce usually going very high in the air.

Clean the bases. When a batter drives in all of the baserunners with a hit.

Clean-up hitter. The fourth batter in the lineup.

Collar. A batter is said to wear this if he has no hits in a game.

Conference. When a coach goes to the mound to talk to his pitcher.

Corks one. Term meaning to hit a long fly ball.

Count. The number of balls and strikes charged to a batter during one at bat.

Crossed him up. When a pitcher threw a pitch other than what the catcher was expecting.

Crossed up. When a pitcher and catcher each think a different pitch is to be thrown.

Curtain call. When a player comes out of the dugout, following a great accomplishment on the field, to acknowledge the crowd's cheers.

Cut down. To be thrown out while baserunning.

Cut-off man. An infielder who positions himself about halfway between the outfielder throwing the ball and base he is throwing to; the infielder cuts off the throw if the ball is off line or will not make it to the target in time to get the baserunner out.

Cutter. A pitcher that moves at the last instant, like a slider.

Cycle. A batter who hits a home run, triple, double, and single in one game.

Decision. When a pitcher of record gets a win or a loss.

Deek. Short for decoy, to fake or fool the opposition.

Delivery. The motion of throwing a pitch.

Deuces wild. A count of two balls, two strikes, and two outs.

Diamond. A baseball field.

Ding-dong. Slang term for a home run.

Dinger. Slang term for a home run.

Doctor the baseball. When a pitcher purposely cuts or disfigures a baseball or puts any illegal substance (i.e., spit or Vaseline) on the ball to give himself an unfair advantage.

Doctor the bat. When a batter illegally alters a bat (i.e., with cork or pine tar).

Dogging it. When a player loafs or he is being lazy on a play.

Double dip. Term for 1) a double-header, and 2) a double play.

Doubled off. When a baserunner is caught in a double play.

Doubleheader. When the same two teams play two games back-to-back on the same day.

Double switch. A lineup change in which a new pitcher and fielder come into the game and the pitcher assumes the position in the batting order farthest away from the current hitter.

Downhill. A phrase yelled at a pitcher to remind him to follow through.

DP. An abbreviation for double plays.

Drag. Short for drag bunt; a bunt attempted for a base hit.

Dribbler. A weakly hit ground ball that goes through the infield for a hit.

Dropped off the table. Expression used to describe an outstanding curveball.

Ducks on the pond. Term used when the bases are loaded.

Dying quail. A softly hit fly ball.

Excuse me swing. Term for a weak swing; much like a check swing.

Extra innings. When a game is tied after nine complete innings, the game goes into extra innings until a winner is determined.

Eye black. The black substance applied under the players' eyes to help reduce glare from the sun.

Face the music. Expression used when a player enters a tough situation and is expected to come through in the clutch.

Fielder's choice. An offensive statistic given to a hitter who reaches base on a play other than a hit or an error.

Find a hole. To hit the ball where the fielders aren't positioned.

Five-tool player. Term for a prospect who is said to possess all five tools needed in professional baseball: 1) running speed, 2) arm strength, 3) ability to hit for power, 4) ability to hit for average, and 5) fielding ability.

Flair. A softly hit ball.

Flame-thrower. A player who throws very hard.

Flash the signs. Description for when a coach is giving signals to players.

Fly out. When a batter hits a fly ball that is caught for an out.

Forkball. A split-finger fastball that is slower than a fastball and usually drops right at the plate.

Foul pole. The poles along the right and left field foul lines that help determine whether a ball is fair or foul.

Foul tip. A ball that barely hits the bat during a swing and then flies toward the catcher.

Four-bagger. A home run.

Free pass. A base on balls.

Front-runner. A player who is great when his team is ahead, but chokes when his team is losing.

Frozen rope. Expression describing an exceptionally hard hit ball.

Fungo bat. A long, slim bat used to hit practice balls to fielders.

Fungoes. A name for practice balls hit to fielders.

Game face. A stern, concentrating look on the face of a player.

Gamer. A name for a player who steps up and plays his best in key situations.

Gas. A pitch thrown very hard.

Go right at him. A phrase yelled at a pitcher to encourage him to just throw strikes and not try to the corners.

Go with the pitch. When a batter hits an outside pitch to the opposite field.

Go yard. Hit a home run.

Grand slam. A home run hit with the bases loaded, thereby scoring four runs.

Grandstand. The seats behind home plate and down the baselines.

Granny. Term meaning a grand slam.

Grooved. Term describing a pitch thrown right down the middle.

Heat. Slang for a ball thrown very hard.

High heat. A fastball up in the zone.

Hit-and-run. An offensive play in which the baserunner(s) take off running and the batter is responsible for hitting the ball on the ground to the right side to avoid the baserunner(s) getting thrown out.

Hitter's count. When a hitter has the pitch count in his favor.

Hold him on. When an infielder, usually a first baseman, stands next to a base that has a baserunner on it to help keep the baserunner's lead to a minimum due to the threat of the pitcher throwing to the base.

Hole in his swing. Term referring to the place in the strike zone where a batter is vulnerable.

Hook. Slang for a curveball.

Hot corner. Common term for third base.

Inside-the-park home run. When a batter hits a home run without the ball going over the outfield fence.

Intentional walk. When a pitcher deliberately walks a batter.

Jack. A home run.

Keystone. Slang for second base.

Lead. Short for leadoff.

Line drive. A hard hit ball with very little arc.

Live arm. Term for a player with great arm strength.

Loaded bat. A wooden bat that has had cork added to the core of the wood to make the ball travel farther.

Meat of the order. The third, fourth, and fifth batters in a batting order.

Mental lapse. When a player makes a mistake, as a result of a lack of focus.

Miscue. An error.

Mix speeds. To throw pitches at various speeds in order to keep the batter off balance.

Mound. The mounded area of dirt where the pitcher stands to pitch.

No-no. Slang for a no hitter.

Nubber. Slang for a ball hit very softly.

Obstruction. When a fielder, who is not in the process of making a play or not in possession of the ball, hinders the advancement of a runner.

Off-speed delivery. Term for any pitch other than a fastball.

On a tear. A phrase used when a player is hitting the ball exceptionally well.

On deck. The batter scheduled to hit after the current batter.

One in the well. To get the first out.

On the ropes. A pitcher on the verge of being knocked out of a game.

Overthrow. When a player throws a ball over his intended target.

Park it. To hit a home run.

Pepper. A short game of throw and hit; generally played during warm-ups.

Perfect game. A game in which one team has no runs, hits, errors, or walks.

Pinch hitter. A substitute batter.

Pinch runner. A substitute runner.

Pine tar. Substance put on a bat to help hitters get a better grip.

Pitch around him. When a team avoids pitching to a dangerous hitter by intentionally walking him.

Pitch count. The number of pitches a pitcher has thrown in a game.

Pitcher of record. The two pitchers who, at any given time in a game, are responsible for either a win or a loss.

Pitching staff. All of the pitchers on a baseball team.

Pitch out. When a pitcher intentionally throws the ball extremely far outside so the catcher can be unimpeded in trying to throw out a baserunner attempting to steal a base.

Plunked. Slang for being hit by a pitch.

Power alleys. Term for left-center and right-center field.

Pull hitter. A batter who tends to pull the ball the majority of the time he hits.

Punch out. To be called out looking.

Put out. When a defensive player records an out.

Quality start. A good pitching performance generally thought of as pitching a minimum of six innings and allowing three or less earned runs in a nine-inning game.

Rabbit ball. Term for a ball that goes a long way when hit.

Rabbit ears. Slang for an umpire who listens to the fans, coaches, and players too much, instead of concentrating on his job.

Rainmaker. A fly ball that is hit very high.

Relief pitcher. A pitcher from the bullpen who enters a game after the starting pitcher or another pitcher is removed.

Retire the side. When the defense records the third out of an inning.

Ribbies. Slang for runs batted in.

Rifle arm. Term for a player with a strong throwing arm.

Roll it over. To turn a double play.

Rubber. The white pitching plate on the pitcher's mound.

Run. The basic unit of scoring in baseball.

Rung up. To strike out looking.

Second sacker. The second baseman.

Serve it up. To give up a home run.

Set-up man. A middle reliever who pitches before the team's closer comes in.

Shelled. A pitcher whose pitches are getting hit very hard.

Shut out. A game where the opposing team does not score a run.

Side is retired. When three outs are made by the defense in an inning.

Signal caller. A catcher.

Sinker. A type of breaking ball that literally sinks when it gets near the plate.

Skipper. A manager or head coach of a baseball team.

Slab. Slang for the pitcher's rubber.

Slice. When a ball is hit down the foul line of the opposite field.

Slide. Term for 1) a losing streak, or 2) a way a baserunner approaches a base to avoid a tag by scooting on his butt, feet first, or on his belly, head first.

Slider. A type of breaking pitch that sinks down and away or down and in to batters.

Slugfest. Term for a very high scoring baseball game.

Slurve. A breaking pitch that is half slider and half curve.

Small ball. Strategic emphasis on bunting, stealing, and the hit and run; trying to play for one run at a time.

Snap throw. A quick pick-off move to first base by a left-handed pitcher.

Solo job. A home run with no one on base.

Southpaw. A left-handed player.

Staff. All of the pitchers on a baseball team; short for pitching staff.

Stanza. An inning.

Stone hands. Term for a poor fielder who tends to have a lot of balls bounce off his glove.

Stranded. When runners are left on base.

Stuff. Term for all of a pitcher's pitches.

Swipe. Term meaning to steal a base.

Switch hitter. A player who can bat right-handed or left-handed.

Take the field. When players run onto the field, ready to play.

Take the mound. When a pitcher gets on the mound, ready to pitch.

Talk smack. To talk trash.

Target. When a catcher holds up his mitt to show the pitcher where he wants him to throw the ball.

Tater. A home run.

Third sacker. The third baseman.

Three-bagger. A triple.

Three in the well. Three outs.

Toe the rubber. When a pitcher makes contact with the pitching rubber.

Tools of ignorance. Slang for the catcher's equipment.

True hop. A ground ball that normal hops and is easier to field.

Twin killing. A double play.

Two-bagger. A double.

Two-seamer. A type of grip used by a pitcher in which he holds his index and middle fingers on two seams of the baseball.

Utility man. A player who can play several different positions.

Walk off home run. A home run hit by a player on the home team that instantly wins the game.

Went yard. Hit a home run.

Whiffed. To strike out.

Wind up. The pitching motion of a pitcher when no one is on base.

Work the count. When a hitter forces a pitcher to throw a lot of pitches in an at bat.

Zip on the ball. Velocity on the ball.

C

Baseball Abbreviations

This appendix provides a listing of selected abbreviations that are commonly used in baseball.

A. Assists

AB. At bats

AB/HR. The ratio of home runs per at bats

AB/K. The ratio of strikouts per at bats

Avg. Batting average (hits divided by at bats)

BB. Base on balls

BF/9. Batters faced per nine innings

BF. Batters faced

BP. Batting practice

CG. Complete games

CGL. Complete game losses

CH. Chances (number of balls hit to a particular player)

CS. Caught stealing

DP. Double plays

E. 1) An error, or 2) term yelled at an opponent when he makes an error

E1. An error on the pitcher

E2. An error on the catcher

E3. An error on the first baseman

E4. An error on the second baseman

E5. An error on the third baseman

E6. An error on the shortstop

E7. An error on the left fielder

E8. An error on the center fielder

E9. An error on the right fielder

EH. Extra hitter. Occasionally used in youth baseball instead of a designated hitter.

ER. Earned runs

ERA. Earned run average (number of earned runs divided by the number of innings pitches times nine)

FLD%. Fielding percentage (putouts added to assists and then divided by the total number of putouts, assists, and errors)

FPCT. Fielding percentage

FPS. First pitch strike

G. Games pitched or games played

GDP. Grounded into a double play

GF. Games finished

GS. Games started

GSH. Grand slam home run

H. Hits and hits allowed

HP/PA. Hit pitches per at bat

HR. Home runs and home runs allowed

IBB. Intentional base on balls

IP. Innings pitched

IPS. Innings per start

IRA. Inherited runs allowed

K. Symbol for a strike out

L. A loss

LOB. Runners left on base

MVP. Most valuable player

NP. Number of pitches

PA. Plate appearances

PB. Passed balls

PK. Pick-offs

R. Runs or runs allowed

RBI. 1) runs batted in, and 2) revitalizing baseball in the inner cities

RPF. Relief failures

S. Saves

SB. Stolen bases

SB%. Stolen base percentage (stolen bases divided by stolen bases + caught stealing)

SF. Sacrifice fly

SH. Sacrifice hits and sacrifice hits allowed

SO. Strikouts

SV. Saves

SVO. Save opportunities

2B. 1) a double, and 2) a second baseman

3B. 1) a triple, and 2) a third baseman

TBF. Total batters faced

TC. Total chances

TP. Triple plays

XBH. Extra base hits

D

Diamond Mom's Equipment Shopping List

■ A Word About Aluminum Bats

Balls that are struck with lightweight aluminum bats can travel faster than those hit off wood bats. This factor poses a potential risk to pitchers and infielders (and even spectators) because the speed and power of the ball can cause injuries if the player cannot respond quickly to the oncoming ball or move from its flight path, especially when the path of the ball is toward his head. Aluminum bats can propel a ball into space at dangerously high speeds, especially if the bat's length is not in proper proportion to its weight. Prior to NCAA regulating the size and weight distribution of these bats, hit balls were found to have traveled at speeds of over 100 mph.

Because of this potentially dangerous situation, the NCAA adopted rules in 2001 to limit bat performances for college baseball. The National Federation of State High School Associations (NFHS) followed suit in the same year and applied the following rules to high school varsity and junior varsity players:

- The bat must be no lighter than three ounces less than its length (also known as -3, e.g., a 33-inch bat cannot weigh less than 30 ounces, or 33/30).

- The barrel must be no more than 2 5/8 inches in diameter.

- All high school bats must also be BESR (Ball Exit Speed Ratio) approved, meaning the ball cannot leave the bat at a speed faster than 97 mph.

Since younger players will have to eventually adjust to using the prescribed aluminum bats, it makes sense to get them used to the feel of this weight/length differential early…and it makes the game safer. This factor is not critical for younger, less powerful players, but it can be important if your son is larger and stronger than other boys of his age.

The durability of aluminum bats is undependable. Even the most expensive ones can break open like a soda can or lose their "ping" and go flat. Should either of these circumstances occur, you would have to replace the bat. Some manufacturers offer a one-time replacement of damaged or flat bats within one year of purchase. Because some manufacturers are no longer offering replacements, you should ask about the replacement policy when purchasing a bat for your son.

■ Buying Guide for Aluminum Bats for High School Players

When purchasing a bat for your son, your son's height and weight should be considered. The following bat guidelines could be employed:

- High school player, freshman year – 31/28
- High school player, sophomore year – 32/29
- High school player, junior to college – 33/30

It should be noted that some manufacturers make larger-sized aluminum bats. On the other hand, few players use them. The player using such a bat would have to be extremely strong to be an effective hitter with one.

■ Shopping List for T-Ball (ages 5-6)

- Baseball shoes with rubber cleats
- Baseball glove—vinyl or soft rubber ($20)
- Aluminum bat (lightest he can hold: $30-$100)
- Equipment bag for holding the above items
- Baseball pants (usually with elastic waist, so no belt is required)
- Socks (team color)
- Belt (team color)
- Sunscreen

Optional accessories:

- Batting gloves
- Sweat bands
- Batting helmet (check with league for specifications)

(Beware of too many accessories at this age; it can make your son feel conspicuous.)

■ Shopping List for Community-Sponsored Youth Leagues (ages 7-12)

- Baseball shoes with rubber cleats
- Baseball glove (leather, medium grade, $50 and up) or catcher's mitt (note difference between the terms "mitt" and "glove")
- Aluminum bat (sized by length/weight; $100-$300)
  - √ Bat length should equal distance from ground to waist of player
  - √ Lightest weight or using -3 as a guideline

- Batting gloves
- Equipment bag for holding the above items
- Baseball pants (consistent with team requirements)
- Socks (team colors; buy lots of socks)
- Belt (team colors; recommend two)
- Sleeves (a long-sleeved T-shirt to wear under uniform in cold weather; sleeves should be team color or neutral color)
- Jock strap and cup (sized youth to adult in sizes small to extra large)
- Sunscreen
- Optional accessories:
- Sliding shorts
- Batting helmet (check with league for specifications)

■ Shopping List for Travel/Elite Baseball and Older Youth Baseball

Refer to the shopping list for *Community-Sponsored Youth Leagues*. Some travel/elite teams have sponsors that provide part of the equipment. The first and foremost rule concerning equipment, is to make sure your son is outfitted with what is necessary for him to play the game safely. When players are 13 years and older, some leagues allow metal cleats. If your son's team plays teams from different leagues, you may want to own a pair of both rubber and metal cleats in the event you play a game where only rubber cleats are allowed. This approach can be a pricy solution, since shoes for players this age can run as high as $100 a pair.

■ Shopping List for High School Baseball

Depending upon the high school your son attends, he may or may not be provided with clothing and equipment from booster clubs and sponsors. The following list of equipment is a guideline. Almost certainly, you will need to buy the first six items on the list.

- Baseball shoes with cleats specified by league rules
- Baseball glove, leather, highest grade ($100 and up)
    - √ First baseman's mitt (note different designation than "glove")
    - √ Infielder's glove (small pocket, shorter)
    - √ Outfielder's glove (deeper pocket, longer)
    - √ Pitcher's glove (no glove exists specifically for pitchers; however, most pitchers want to use a glove that is closed or hides the ball from the batter)

√ Catcher's mitt (note different designation than "glove")

- Aluminum bat (sized by length/weight using -3 as the guideline; price range $100 to $300)
- Baseball pants for practice and/or to complete uniform (check team requirements for color; two pairs are recommended)
- Socks (team color; buy lots of socks)
- Sleeves (a long-sleeved T-shirt to wear under uniform in cold weather; color of sleeves should be team color or neutral color)
- Belt (team color—two are recommend)
- Batting gloves
- Jock strap and cup (sized youth to adult in sizes small to extra large)
- Equipment bag
- Sunscreen

Optional accessories:

- Sliding shorts
- Batting helmet (check with league for specifications)

Many thanks to Danny Tussy at Chicks Sporting Goods in Oceanside, California, for helping create the Diamond Moms Equipment Shopping List.

Vitamins and Supplements Shopping List*

Multiple vitamins (*all ages*). Multiple vitamins for children tend to be the same for boys and girls; once your son is 15 years or older, purchase multiple vitamins for men; look for "food-based" multiple vitamins (i.e., vitamins made from whole foods) whenever possible.

Vitamin C (*all ages*). Ester-C is preferred because it is easy on the stomach; best taken with food.

Essential fatty acid supplement (*all ages*). A combination of omega 3, 6, and 9 oils is preferred.

Flax seed oil or flakes (*all ages*). Helps with elimination.

Food enzymes (*all ages*). Refer to chapter 15 for specific information.

Probiotics (all ages). Types found in refrigerator section preferred; combination of acidophilus and bifidus recommended.

Green foods (*all ages*)

Protein powders (*all ages*). Brands with low sugar preferred.

Glucosamine and chondroitin combination (*older players only*). Good for players who do repetitive motion (e.g., pitchers and catchers); can also help players who are recovering from injury.

CoEnzyme Q-10 (*older players only*). Suspended in flax or vitamin E oil.

---

* This list is based on my personal recommendations. You should consult with a registered dietician or physician prior to implementing any changes in your diet or health regimen.

F

Contacting Colleges and Coaches

(for or by your son)

Applying to schools for admission and communicating with the coaches of those schools is not unlike applying for a job. Like all employers, the school or coach of choice is looking for the very best applicant. Your first impression is most often the most important. If a poor impression is made, it can be very difficult to regain ground. More often than not, the first impression a school or coach will get is the one delivered through snail mail or e-mail. Entering college is serious business because, it is just that…a business.

As you prepare your correspondence, first make sure you have the right names of the coaching staff (head coach and assistants) and that you are sending the communication to the right person. It is especially important that you check spellings and make sure you have the correct address. Double- and triple-proofread your work to make sure there are no typographical errors or incomplete sentences in the text. Have someone you trust and respect look over the letter with you.

The form for the letter should be that of a traditional business letter. An outline of a sample letter is detailed in this appendix, using what is known as a "block form." This letter includes italicized sections offering ideas and suggestions for inputting information particular to you as an individual. In addition to the sample form letter, this appendix also offers a completed letter, written to a fictitious college from a fictitious applicant. These letters are only suggestions, which you can use if you so choose. However, you are encouraged to make your letter reflect your personality. Help the coaches know who you are not just as a student athlete, but also as an individual.

While it is important for you to state the facts that support your talent and attributes, make sure you keep the ideas relatively simple, factual, and direct without sounding like a braggart. For instance, telling a coach that you are a dedicated and hard worker is a good thing, especially when your high school coaches and/or teachers can back that information up. But to tell a coach you are the best player in the state in which you live…well, that is way over the top, if it is not, in fact, true. Be honest; toot your horn, but don't blast it.

Sample Form Letter

Your name
Street address and apartment number, if applicable
City, state, zip code
Telephone number

E-mail address

Date of letter

Name of coach with title (e.g. John Smith, Head Baseball Coach)
Athletic department
College (university of any city)
Address
City, state, zip code

Dear Coach Smith:

I would like to take this opportunity to introduce myself to you. My name is _____ and I am currently a _____ (*current grade*) at _____ (*name of school*). I play _____ (*position*) for my high school's baseball team and have been a varsity player for ____ years.

I have researched colleges and I am interested in attending your university as a student and as a baseball player. (*At this point you can add other pertinent information, such as that one of your parents graduated from this school, or that you have always wanted to attend this school, or any other information you feel would catch the coach's interest.*) I have enclosed a copy of my athletic resume and a list of references. (*References should include names and addresses and other pertinent contact information, such as e-mail or phone number of coaches (current and past) and academic advisers or teachers. You can also include the name of an adult who has had a substantial influence on your life, such as an employer, minister, or conditioning coach or trainer.*)

I will be playing for _____ (*team*) this summer and I have listed my travel coach on my list of references. I have also been invited to and will attend the _____ Showcase in _____ (*month*) in (*city and state*) on (*date*).

I feel I would be an asset to your team because I am (*a good baseball player who works hard, dedicated to my personal pursuit of excellence, loyal, enthusiastic…give the coach a sense of your confidence without sounding overly obnoxious.*) I can be reached at the address or numbers listed above. Please let me know if you require further information or have any questions. Thank you for taking the time to review my letter and resume.

Sincerely,

Darn Good Player

Sample Completed Letter

James Wood
1234 Awesome Avenue
Homerun, FL 12345
123-456-7890
jwood1@aol.com

June 15, 2010

John Smith, Head Baseball Coach
Athletic Department
University of Any City
5678 College Avenue
Any City, FL 34567

Dear Coach Smith:

I would like to take this opportunity to introduce myself to you. My name is James Wood and I am currently a junior at James Town High School in Home Run, Florida. I pitch and play third base for the James Town Tornados and I have been a varsity player since my sophomore year.

I have researched colleges and I am interested in attending your university as a student and as a baseball player. While on vacation, my family and I made an informal visit of your campus and I really liked it. I have researched the different options for majors at UAC and feel it offers the kinds of classes that will support my scholastic objectives. I have also followed the success of your baseball team and feel I could contribute in a positive way to its continued success. I have enclosed a copy of my athletic resume and a list of references.

I will be playing in a wood bat league for the Prospects this summer and I have listed my travel coach on my list of references. I have also been invited and will attend the Team One Showcase in Miami on June 27, 2010.

I feel I would be an asset to your team because I am someone who works hard to be the best student and player I can be. I can be reached at the address or numbers listed above. Please let me know if you require further information or have any questions. Thank you for taking the time to review my letter and resume.

Sincerely,

Darn Good Player

G

Parental Resources

■ The National Pitching Association

PO Box 2350

Del Mar, CA 92014

866-977-4824

www.nationalpitching.com

The National Pitching Association is comprised of a team of highly talented management and a coaching staff that works closely with an all-star advisory board. The NPA involves several entities that are dedicated to enhancing the body of knowledge concerning pitching mechanics, conditioning, mental aspects, coaching techniques, diet, and health aspects. As the NPA conducts research into these factors, it channels the information it gains to the public through its schools, camps, products, and informational website. The NPA is committed to helping anyone who wants to coach, play, advise, or support young athletes with as much accurate and up-to-date information as possible

■ Winning Mind

Geoff Miller, MA

619-255-5250

www.thewinningmind.com

Winning Mind, LLC, is a high-performance consulting group dedicated to helping people dramatically improve their ability to perform under pressure and achieve meaningful goals. WM helps organizations and individuals who recognize the importance of human factors in the pursuit of excellence. WM clients include Olympic and professional athletes, the US Army Special Operations Command at Ft. Bragg, and several Fortune 500 executives.

Tom House—Baseball Visionary

"If I had the perfect world, the passion and excitement that little leaguers feel when they show up on the first day would never be diminished; it would only be enhanced."

—Tom House

Every profession has mentors who stand out, and baseball is no exception to that rule. The dictionary defines mentor as someone who is a "trusted counselor or guide; tutor; coach." To have an individual embody all four attributes is indeed a gift. Dr. Tom House is such a man. He is also the person who taught me that baseball is a game of failure, and it was my job as my son's mother to continue to believe in him at all times, particularly on those occasions when he didn't believe in himself. His belief that baseball needs mothers more than mothers need baseball says it all for diamond moms everywhere.

Coming from a background steeped in baseball tradition, Tom played high school baseball in Southern California. He was drafted out of high school but chose to attend the University of Southern California instead. As a left-handed pitcher in 1965 playing for USC, he was profoundly influenced by his baseball coach, the renowned Rod Dedeaux. Tom unabashedly admits that his USC experiences left him deeply blessed to have had the opportunity to be coached by this rare and talented individual.

In 1967, the Braves drafted Tom, and he began a career in the major leagues that lasted over eight years. When he finished his career in the minor leagues upon his release from spring training in 1979, he began his coaching career. Returning to college, he earned a bachelor's degree in business management and an MBA in marketing from USC. Realizing his heart was on the baseball field—not in an office—he went back to school to get an advanced degree in exercise physiology and nutrition. Eventually, he earned a Ph.D. in psychology.

Making a difference is not an easy thing to do in the deeply traditional landscape of baseball. There is often tremendous resistance to change of any kind. It is extremely rare to find experienced individuals in the ranks of baseball who embrace change and evolution. No one has been a more ardent advocate of doing what is best for baseball than Tom. His quest to create the kind of game for our kids that still holds the magical quality of its tradition, but offers forward-thinking and needed change to its infrastructure, is tireless and unceasing.

Among Tom's thoughts on baseball that have become the cornerstones of the National Pitching Association are the following:

■ *On Coaching:*

"Too many coaches put out the fire in players instead of nurturing their talent and ability."

"We have a tendency, as coaches and parents, to take it personally when these kids are not perfect."

■ *On Parenting Concepts:*

"I think it is a must for parents to interview travel coaches…" before signing your son up for a team.

"The one thing I would say to any parent or athlete who is being actively recruited is to trust your heart."

"Be your son's advocate."

■ *On Pitch Counts:*

"Pitch counts should be age-specific."

"It is far better to err on the side of limiting your son to throwing too few pitches than to let him throw too many."

■ *On Training, Travel Teams, and Elite Teams:*

"I think playing baseball is good. In Latin America and the Pacific Rim they play baseball year round. But the problem is that our kids pitch too much and don't throw enough."

"…On weekends, jumping into vans or buses and being transported to throw in a weekend league, while they have done nothing to physically prepare for this during the week, can be devastating on a young arm."

■ *On College Recruiting:*

"College recruiting, like professional scouting, is a business … I don't think that many parents realize that it is just that…"

"Look at the landscape and pick what is right for your situation."

■ *On Moms and Baseball:*

"Baseball needs moms a whole lot more than moms need baseball."

■ *On Enhancement Drugs:*

"The NPA strongly recommends that athletes do not take steroids or enhancement drugs."

"The NPA believes that using enhancement drugs represents a very poor choice for an athlete."

The National Pitching Association, under the leadership of Dr. Tom House, emphasizes four objectives based upon information, instruction, and inspiration. All of its programs are based on what Tom refers to as the four M's:

- Master information
- Mentor a kid
- Make a difference
- Move on from there

Each person on his NPA staff is held to these noteworthy standards. This NPA's no-nonsense approach to working with kids is something from which we can all learn. We are, after all, the most important coach to our son. We are his *life* coach.

Cited References

Allen, Jane. Personal interview. 8 Mar. 2005.

Anabolic Steroid Abuse. Spring 2005. www.steroidabuse.org.

Carroll, Will. *Saving the Pitcher*. Chicago, Illinois: Ivan R. Dee, 2004.

Drug Abuse. Spring 2005. www.drugabuse.gov.

Feingold. Spring 2005. www.feingold.org.

Filter (Coach), Rusty. San Diego State University. Personal interview. 29 Feb. 2005.

Frank, Noah. Personal interview. 19 Feb. 2005.

Giles, Monica. Telephone interview. 16 Feb. 2005.

Gwynn (Coach), Tony. San Diego State University. Personal interview. 28 Feb. 2005.

Harmon, Dawn. NAIA. Personal interview. 20 Apr. 2005.

Healthy Living. 13 Mar. 2005. www.healthyliving.org.

Herbold (Coach), John. Personal interview. 12 Apr. 2005.

Hoorelbeke, Dabar. Personal interview. 25 May 2005

House (Coach), Tom. Telephone and e-mail interview. 2 Dec. 2005.

Johnson (Coach), Dominick. Personal interview. 29 Apr. 2005.

The Language of Baseball. Monterey, CA: Coaches Choice, 2002.

Lysander, Rick. Personal interview. 23 Mar. 2005.

Lysander, Tracey. Personal interview. 9 Apr. 2005.

Miller, Geoff. Telephone interview. 12 Jan. 2005.

Moore (Coach), Greg. "University of San Francisco, question for book." E-mail to Coach Moore. 18 May 2005.

Morgan, Lally and Richard, Joe. *Baseball for Dummies, 3rd Edition*. Hoboken, NJ: Wiley Publishing Inc., 2005.

National Association of Intercollegiate Athletics. 19 Apr. 2005. www.naia.org.

National Pitching Association. 17 Nov. 2004. www.nationalpitching.com.

NCAA. 21 Apr. 2005. www2.ncaa.org.

NCAA Clearing House. 21 Apr. 2005. www.ncaaclearinghouse.net.

PamRotella.com. 23 May 2005. www.goodfats.pamrotella.com.

Peale, Judy. Survey and personal interview. 12 Feb. 2005.

Preisenderfer, Angie. Survey by mail interview. 5 Mar. 2005.

Pro Baseball Tryouts. 31 June 2005. www.probaseballtryouts.com.

Prorank International Baseball Services. 24 Apr. 2005. www.prorank.net.

Renkins, Jack. *Recruiting Realities*. Scottsdale, AZ: Brookes & John Publishing, 2001.

Stanley, Ellen. Personal interview. 23 Feb. 2005.

Super Size Me. 13 May 2005. www.supersizeme.com

Taylor (Associate Director of Athletics), Wendy. University of San Diego. Telephone interview. 14 Apr. 2005.

USA Baseball. 14 Apr. 2005. www.usabaseball.com.

US Department of Human Services and SAMHSA's National Clearing House Alcohol & Drug Information. Spring 2005. www.health.org.

Weissman (Coach), Craig. Telephone interview. 29 Apr. 2005.

Winning Mind. 9 Feb. 2005. www.thewiningmind.com.

Recommended References

The resource information available on parenting, coaching, and learning is quite varied. As a Diamond Mom, finding the right fit when it comes to instruction can be a daunting task when faced with so much variety. The books, DVDs/videos, and materials included in this appendix are ones in which I have confidence. Depending upon your interests and circumstances, they can be valuable for you, as a mother, and for your son, as an athlete. My publisher's website, www.coacheschoice.com, also offers an exceptional array of resources in which you might be interested. Coaches Choice offers instructional books, hands-on teaching videos, and in-their-own-words clinic lecture videos, featuring edited presentations by some of the best known coaches in their sport.

Another very useful source of materials that can help you is the National Pitching Association website, www.nationalpitching.com, which markets DVDs, videos, and books featuring Dr. Tom House.

- *On Pitching:*

  Bennett, B. (1997). Pitching from the Ground Up. Monterey, CA: Coaches Choice

  Carroll, W. (2004). *Saving the Pitcher*. Chicago, IL: Ivan R. Dee

  House, T. Reddick, P. (2003). *The Pitcher Perfect Pitcher*. Monterey, CA: Coaches Choice

- *On Hitting:*

  Gwynn, T. and Vaughn, R. (1998). *The Art of Hitting. New York*, NY: GT Publishing.

  Lau, C., Glosbrenner., LaRussa, T. (1986). *The Art of Hitting* 300. New York, NY: Penguin Books USA Inc.

  Ortiz, L. (2005). *The Natural Hitter*. Monterey, CA: Coaches Choice.

  Schmidt, M., Ellis, R. (1994). *The Mike Schmidt Study: Hitting, Theory, Skills, and Technique*. Atlanta, GA: McGriff & Bell Inc.

  Williams, T. Underwood, J. (1986). *The Science of Hitting*. New York, NY: Simon & Schuster, Inc.

- *Inspirational/Instructional:*

  Brown, B. (2002). 1001 *Motivational Quotes and Messages*. Monterey, CA: Coaches Choice.

  Dorfman, H. and Kuhel, K. (1994, 2000). *The Mental Game of Baseball: A Guide to Peak Performance*. South Bend, IN: Diamond Communications, Inc.

  Jamison, S. and Tiano, A. (2000). *John Wooden Values, Victory, and Peace of Mind*. (VHS) Steve Jamison Productions.

  Maffetone, P. (2000). *The Maffetone Method, The Holistic, Low-Stress, No-Pain Way to Exceptional Fitness*. Camden, ME: Ragged Mountain Press

- *College and Recruiting Resources and Tools:*

  Kadupski, C. (revised annually). *The Sport Source, Official Athletic College Guide*. Dallas, TX: Charlie Kadupski.

  Renkens, J. (2003). *Recruiting Realities*. Scottsdale, AZ: Brookes and John Publishing.

  The Calendar Coach (2004-2005). Kalendarium Incorporated (10/2005). www.thekalendarium.com.

- *Parenting:*

  Biddulph, S. (2002). *The Secret of Happy Children*. New York, NY: MJF Books.

  Glenn, S. (2000). *Raising Self-Reliant Children in a Self-Indulgent World*. Roseville, CA: Prima Publishing

  Rosenberg. M. (2003). *Non-Violent Communication, a Language of Life*. Encinitas, CA: PuddleDancer Press

  Zaillian, S. (director). Searching for Bobby Fischer (movie), Hollywood, CA: Mirage Entertainment.

All materials listed are available on Amazon.com, another great resource for other baseball-related titles.

About the Author

Candace Conradi is an author, entrepreneur, and Diamond Mom. For the past 15 years, Candace has been team mother for a variety of teams, served on her son's high school baseball booster board, worked on baseball fundraisers, and co-founded Legit Sports, Inc. (www.legitsportsinc.com), a company that produces a pitcher's training device.

Candace has four children ranging in ages from 20 to 33 and is passionate about her role as a mom. When her youngest son, Stephen, was two years old, she noticed extraordinary signs of athleticism. Stephen began playing soccer when he was four years old and did so until he was 10. While he experimented with other sports, such as basketball, football, and golf, it was baseball that caught his attention. By the age of 10, he had fallen in love with baseball. Recognizing his passion and talent, Candace and her husband decided they would do whatever they could to help him develop his natural ability.